TO FATHER AN AMERICAN CHAMPION

Mr. James E. Kovacevich
5616 SW Charlestown St
Seattle WA 98116

A Father's Guide

James E. Kovacevich

5616 S.W. Charlestown St. • Seattle, WA 98116

Home: (206) 932-7477 • Cell: (206) 396-5908

E-Mail: RLK2k@aol.com

Stephen L. Doherty

Printed in the United States of America.

Cover design by Steve Riecks

ISBN 0-9744502-0-0

American Champion Publishing
9227 Lincoln Avenue, Suite 200
Lone Tree, CO 80124

DEDICATION

To my warm and beautiful wife, Tanya,

my beloved son, Braden, and my

sweet baby daughter, Julia.

Fifty years from now it will not
Matter what kind of car you drove,
What kind of house you lived in,
How much money you had in your bank
Account, or what your clothes looked like.
But the world may be a little better
Because you were important
In the life of a child....

—Anonymous

ACKNOWLEDGEMENTS

I would like to acknowledge everyone who contributed to this book, directly or indirectly. Without their assistance, counsel, input, guidance, or cooperation, this book would not have been possible. I especially would like to acknowledge these wonderful people...

Tanya Doherty

My wife. Success is not possible without the love and support of your family. In her own gentle manner, Tanya gave me the continued inspiration and support to accomplish this project. I owe her so much that I can never repay—but I'm going to try anyway.

Tom and Suzanne Dutcher

I couldn't wish for more loving and supportive in-laws than these. Truth be told, this book is a mirror representation of the ideals and inherent values in their respective family trees. They were this book's first fans and kept my embers burning to see the project through.

James and Mary Doherty

My parents. Although they are now deceased, their unique stewardship of my character and values is proof positive that good seeds, if planted young, will eventually take root and blossom.

Millie Limbaugh

When I made the decision to write this book, Millie Limbaugh was my first phone call. We became friends and remained such until her passing three years ago. I found her input invaluable and her perspective on her husband and family fascinating and enjoyable. Millie's family epitomizes the virtues promoted in this book and I will never forget her.

Richard and Joe Kovacevich

As the CEO of Wells Fargo, Richard Kovacevich is, arguably, America's greatest banker. His kindness and consideration, as the first subject I interviewed for this book, was the catalyst for this project and gave it the legitimacy necessary to get started. His father, Joe, spent hours sharing with me his thoughts and philosophies on fathering. He and Dick are shining examples of the love and dedication required to raise true champions. Much of Wells Fargo's success can be directly linked to Dick Kovacevich's personal integrity and core values and convictions. Interestingly, the elements of the corporate culture at Wells Fargo are better represented in this book than in most business texts.

The Joe Dumars Family

As a professional basketball player with the Detroit Pistons, Joe Dumars was a throwback to the days of Russell and Cousy, when talent and performance, not bombast and flamboyance, were the truest measures of the man. Joe was routinely recognized with awards denoting leadership and good sportsmanship. I want to thank the Dumars family for inviting me into their home and sharing their memories of Joe Dumars Senior. Though deceased, his legacy of kindness and caring for children extends far enough to touch my family and my children. As a father, he had few equals and is still the model I would hold up as the standard for decency, caring, and kindness.

Mike Utley

A special thanks and tribute to Mike Utley. Once a former all-pro lineman with the Detroit Lions, a paralyzing on-field injury left him permanently paralyzed, from the waist down, and confined to a wheelchair. But Mike Utley is a warrior and has fought his way back to the edge of mobility. His accomplishments since his injury are every bit as impressive as his performance on the football field. Whenever I feel down or think things are tough, one quick thought of Mike and I'm almost embarrassed I felt that way in the first place. He has been a special inspiration to me and I sincerely believe he will be the first spinal paralysis victim to overcome this obstacle and walk again.

Jack Elway

I didn't get to spend a lot of time with Jack, father of Denver Bronco quarterback John Elway, but it was clear to me from the outset that he feels the values and lessons in this book were the right ones for fathers seeking the best for their children. His input was consistent with other great fathers and his kids did okay.

John Wooden

I found him a humble and gracious man of kindness whose sole motivation is his love for the people in his life. I feel fortunate to know him and grateful for the kindness and consideration he extended me, an unknown person to him, in sharing his home and his thoughts so considerately. He's a great American and a wonderful teacher and father.

Given the tremendous impact he had on my life in but a few short hours—I marvel at what having him as teacher, coach, mentor, and friend must have been like for his basketball players at UCLA. Judging from their comments and memories of their days under Coach Wooden, they clearly feel the same way.

CONTENTS

PREFACE

Father, Daddy, Papa . . . he's known to us by many names, all of which conjure up special memories...and feelings...of his role in our lives. This book is a personal dedication and salute to fathers and to fatherhood. I hope it motivates today's fathers to reassert their traditional role in the American family. The chapters are a combination of my own personal experience and input from some great American fathers. Their stories illustrate the most important lessons a father can teach his kids. Lessons that mold character and shape destinies.

The book also should encourage anyone with children, or anyone thinking of having children, to truly understand what's at stake when they bring a new life into the world. It's been oft said, *"Anyone can make a baby, but not everyone can be a father!"* My hope is that this book will do more than make men *try* to be better fathers. I hope that it will make them *want* to be great fathers. Fathers of American Champions...

"Champion" Defined

Champion. A powerful word that stirs differently in all of us. It invokes images of Herculean feats, glorious victories forged in epic battles. To most of us, champions are "winners" who defied all odds and emerged victorious. We worship them, envy their achievements and wish that, just once, we could view the world from their shoes. They are modern-day gladiators acting out the fantasy in all of us to compete and be victorious against all odds. They are today's heroes—tomorrow's legends.

Yet *real* champions embody more important attributes truly worthy of our admiration and respect. Traits like civic contribution, social responsibility, moral character, and strong family values. The truly great champions are responsible and dedicated role models.

Real champions are role models because of *who* they are, not *what* they do. And within this select group the lifelong presence of dedicated fathers was their primary influence. Fathers who provided the necessary guidance to forge the essential building blocks of true character. The <u>true</u> champions are the fathers and grandfathers dedicated to traditional family values consistent with the principles of our Founding Fathers.

The basis for this book is pretty simple: A champion's life does not end at the practice field, the news desk, the competitive arena, or the boardroom...it only *begins* there.

Our most trustworthy stewards, loving and committed fathers, influenced the men and women I interviewed for this book. Fathers who equally valued character and talent. Their reward will come long after they're gone. Their legacy? Their children's lives. Lives remembered more for positive contributions to society than victories in the arena.

This book identifies twelve vital characteristics intrinsic to true "champions." These chapters and their accompanying anecdotes are meant to be enlightening, inspirational, and humorous. They will touch each of you in different ways, but all of you will gain a new sense of urgency and encouragement to raise your children to be true American Champions.

My intent is to castigate ANY father deficient in fulfilling his paternal role and obligation. Only then will strong and stable families reestablish the moral standard for future generations.

To Mothers

Not long ago I grabbed my little kids and declared firmly, "It's about time the two of you knew who the boss is around here...and when she's not home...!" Let me be crystal clear. While this book focuses on things fathers should be doing, it suggests that mothers are still shouldering most of the "heavy lifting." Indisputably, mothers are the glue that binds families together. They are America's beacons providing light to safe harbor for America's children.

* * *

Tonight nearly forty percent of America's children will fall asleep in a fatherless home. They will doze off without the assurance of safety that only a father's presence can guarantee. In many respects, they have been abandoned. With no dependable father, children themselves will become undependable. In a child's world, adult decisions are being forced upon them daily, decisions that no children should have to make for themselves. Our world is too dangerous for young novices to navigate alone without experienced guides.

Chillingly, these hazards no longer restrict themselves to the inner city nor are they exclusive to only families of poverty. Columbine's fury erupted in a six-figure suburban enclave. As a result, armed guards now roam the hallways of America's schools searching for drugs and/or weapons. Kids killing kids has become so commonplace that except for aberrations like Columbine, we scarcely notice. The critical importance of fatherless homes transcends all conventional boundaries. We all are equally vested in this national cultural plague.

No Father Around? Shame on Him!

In record numbers, spineless American men are conceiving children with no more thought or regard than they might exercise fertilizing their lawns. I have little faith in rehabilitating cowards so I choose, rather, to focus on educating patriots and encouraging legitimate American citizens. Let's spend whatever it takes to rescue these offspring. Let's further invest in encouraging future parents to dedicating themselves to raising real American Champions! There's no shame in embracing and promoting American pride, commitment, courage, perseverance, resolve, compassion, and kindness.

To the contrary . . . there is much *honor*.

INTRODUCTION

CHAMPIONS ARE NOT UNIQUE IN AMERICA,
BUT HOW WE RAISE THEM
IS UNIQUELY AMERICAN.

A t no time in our fabled history has this distinction been more important than right now when, once again, we've been placed in history's crosshairs amidst global unrest. And once again the world will experience and understand the unique traits of American champions who not long ago were America's children. No explanation will be required as to why Americans are different. The world will just know.

America is distinct among nations for one reason and one reason only. At its genesis, America adopted a fundamental philosophy that was unparalleled in the annals of history. Even among today's democratic nations, this fundamental edict is rarely acknowledged, let alone held sacrosanct.

In a profound and epic gesture our founding fathers embraced Judeo-Christian doctrine as the pillars of America's burgeoning constitution. Our forefathers held that God bestowed the gift of freedom to *all* mankind. Hence, America wasn't founded on any concept of extending freedom to its citizens. It was crafted so as not to *impede* it! Our forefathers also exhibited exceptional wisdom and foresight by guaranteeing these liberties constitutionally, and pledging to defend them unconditionally. America's strength and solidarity is merely its collective elimination of its restraints.

By contrast, history is rife with examples of impeding and restraining the freedom of the many, on behalf of the appetites and desires of the few. The same freedom God intended for everyone. The world isn't lacking freedom—it's just deficient in restraining those wishing to deny it. The mere concept of *anyone* proclaiming to extend or grant freedom is to place oneself into the shoes of God...impossible but commonly attempted by history's most notorious and oppressive despots.

In today's world, freedom's ring resembles a global lottery. One can only hope to be born into a citizenry that doesn't grant freedom but guarantees it. Unto that purpose America stands, distinctively, alone. Americans understand and respect that God grants no more than man, if he so chooses, will honor and defend.

There is no other coherent argument that remotely explains why America dominates virtually all aspects of global influence. We're no better than the rest of the world. We merely thrive, compete, and prosper in a civilization that is unwavering and vigilant in its protection of the unfettered, God-given human spirit.

Americans Are Different . . . We Are Unique

So why is America unique in its rearing of American champions? It's not complicated. Moral clarity seldom is. All of our nation's children are champions in their own right. Relatively speaking, our worst will always rank among humanity's best. Being raised in a culture where individual dreams have no limitations is a good start.

But our kids *are* different for other important reasons. Their pursuit of greatness is born as much from a sense of purpose as personal recognition; equal part destiny and desire. They come to understand that being an American carries distinct advantages as well as unique obligations and burdens. Their victories will routinely be greeted with as much vilification as idolization. They'll emerge as political targets of criticism as often as legitimate champions and role models. Far from viewing themselves as entitled, America's children—America's champions—bear the additional burden of someday being called on to free yet another generation of enslaved nations...the very countries that today criticize and condemn us. What other nation's fathers gaze upon their infants with the knowledge, and consent, that someday they may be called upon to sacrifice their lives on the behalf of oppressed others?

Too often America is viewed, and judged, internationally as some sort of entitled, elitist country. Predictably, this assessment conveniently ignores the blunt reality that no nation has ever endured more sacrifice or produced more courageous heroes on behalf of history's global victims, than America. Americans are different. Accept it. Deal with it. Someday you may need our help.

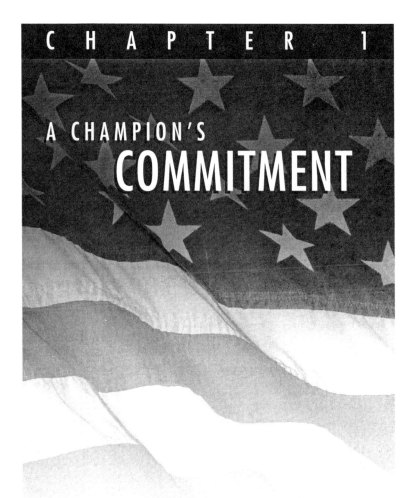

CHAPTER 1

A CHAMPION'S COMMITMENT

*Resolve that whatever you do,
you will bring the whole man to it;
that you will fling the whole
weight of your being into it.*

Orison Swett Marden

Should I or Shouldn't I?

Every community in America has at least one. A shameful reminder of what happens when a commitment proves to be little more than novelty. What am I talking about? I'm talking about those homes we all drive by with disgust. Homes with sad and lonely dogs tethered in the back yard, water bowl empty, stale food stuck to their filthy dishes, and scant shelter to brave the harsh seasons. Wretched and pathetic "former cute puppies," mired in a lonely, hopeless existence. I'm always struck by the same thought—*Why buy a dog, only to subject it to a life of sadness and hopeless misery?*

To Father an American Champion...demands the same answers from parents and prospective parents who carelessly bring babies into the world—only to assign them a comparable fate. Their answers are disturbing. Be it puppy or baby, the reasons are similar. It was cute, novel, fun, and seemed like a really good idea at the time.

What's missing in both instances is *commitment*. Raising American champions requires 100-percent commitment to the development and well-being of your sons and daughters. If you elect fatherhood—nominate commitment. The "conceive and leave" crowd has already deprived enough innocent children of the promise and presence only a father can provide. I think America's children deserve better.

Embracing a newborn baby initiates an extra-ordinary journey...for both of you. From the instant that baby's eyes open and focus on you, every role and responsibility in your life becomes subordinate to just one—father. If you're unable to make this commitment . . . *don't do it!* Take a cold shower or go play pool but don't recklessly conceive yet another neglected child. The gift of a new life is God's most precious gift and a father's most sacred honor. Accepting it assigns an enormous moral obligation and responsibility.

The ability to accept responsibility is the true measure of the man.

—Roy L. Hunt

My Own Father

My own sense of parental purpose and commitment came from my father. His life was neither distinctive nor, by most standards, even successful. But his character embodied distinction and success by the strength of his beliefs and allegiance to his convictions. Bravery, commitment, and courage *is* distinctive.

In 1941 my father was a young and ambitious teenager with his whole life ahead of him—until the Japanese bombed Pearl Harbor. In an instant his youthful plans were forestalled as America was thrust into another World War. Without hesitation, my dad eagerly enlisted in the Air Force and was soon dodging bombs in the Philippines.

So what drove a generation of young Americans into this horrific conflict? My dad was characteristic of most. He abhorred fighting and detested conflict. By nature he was a very gentle and peaceful man, vacant of any prejudice for the Japanese.

He volunteered because he *understood*. He got it—like most young men of his generation "got it." As an American he understood and accepted that it was his turn, like countless generations preceding him, to defend our great nation. Ever faithful to that obligation he instinctively enlisted for combat duty. Pretty cool for a Detroit teenager barely out of high school. He was no less vigilant as a father. He understood. *He got it.*

Commitment was his sole parenting tool. He simply would accept no shortcomings when it came to raising his children. Period. He took very seriously that a father, much like a soldier, has duties and respon-sibilities with considerable long-term ramifications.

The soul would have no rainbow had the eyes no tears.

—John Vance Cheney

Special Moments Matter

Reflecting back on those days that touched our lives brings to mind a special moment.

My father and I attended very few public events together, but they were always special and somber affairs. Why? Unfailingly, when the American flag was

5

raised amidst any rendition of our national anthem—he would instinctively rise and come to attention! His head high, right hand clamped firmly over his heart, he would proudly, and clearly, sing the national anthem. As he sang, tears filled his eyes. It was during these moments when I sensed that his thoughts were far from this event—miles from this arena.

We never discussed nor even acknowledged those tears. Life's most cherished moments defy attempts at reconciliation. They were merely the honest, unabashed and unapologetic tears of one proud and patriotic soldier—a dedicated American. They were tears of sadness for so many lives lost in combat to secure the collective freedom of America's children.

But a single glance my way betrayed the real source of those tears. They were tears of happiness and relief that, just maybe, his actions might spare me, his "baby," the horrific combat duty that nearly took *his* life.

Example is the school of mankind
and they will learn at no other.
—Edmund Burke

The Ultimate Commitment...
Love and Support Mom!

Preaching commitment is one thing. Practicing it is quite another. Few lessons will be as useful to our children as their understanding of the word *commitment.*

So how do we express commitment? By example! We all know parents who practice "Do as I say, not as I do" parenting. This dumbfounds me! Am I the only parent who comprehends that our children hang on our every action and utterance? My own kids resemble miniature video cameras. I no sooner do or say something than, BAM!, they both embrace and implement it!

The best example of commitment is the example *I* set in how I treat their *mother.* My wife and I are as different as night and day, rarely seeing things the same way. It would be easy and natural for us to project an image of perpetual conflict and disagreement to our kids. But we don't. I treat my wife with the respect and dignity she deserves, especially in the presence of my son and daughter. She has assumed a responsibility understood only by other stay-at-home mothers. To this end, my own cooperation and contributions are essential.

I strongly believe that most mothers return to former careers because it's *easier* than staying home with their kids. That's sad and misguided. To those ends, they sacrifice so many priceless moments that can be experienced but once.

How do I know this? A year ago my wife was away visiting her family. I was charged with staying home and caring for my one year old and three year old— for seven straight days! Normally my regular job requires a focused and sustained effort. But after three days with my beloved children, who really are well behaved and easy to be around, I couldn't wait to get back to the *ease and comfort* of my hectic career. Raising kids properly, full-time and all the time, is hands-down the hardest job in America—and the hours and pay stink!

To gain that which is worth having,
It may be necessary to lose everything.
—Bernadette Devlin

If Possible...Stay Home With Them

Unfortunately, in today's culture, advocating or promoting the benefits of stay-at-home moms is seen as out of step or out of vogue. Clearly, and understandably, many families require two incomes to survive. There's no sin or shame in that.

Nevertheless, far too many mothers don't need the money but are simply unwilling to make the necessary sacrifices to ensure full-time parental companionship for their children.

Give me a child for the first seven years,
and you may do what you like with him
afterward.
—Source Unknown

Consider Your Choices Carefully

Mothers everywhere—you owe it to yourself, and to your baby, to give this careful thought when deciding to have children. If there's any way you can swing it, reward yourself and compensate your kids by staying home—at *least* for the first five to seven years, when they so desperately need your time and attention. No job can provide the satisfaction of giving the world a happy, successful, and well-adjusted adult.

An unexpectedly rewarding outcome of devoting our lives to our children is how easily and naturally they learn and develop in an environment designed *specifically* for that purpose. When kids know, really know, that their world is OK and that your love and devotion will always be there—it's amazing how they blossom! Their natural instincts, abilities, curiosities, and unique individual gifts advance beautifully in this *made to order* environment, expressly designed to enhance their progress.

But don't push them! I think most of us would agree that ALL kids would be better off without the loud-mouth jerk sports parents. They're not hard to spot. They're the raving idiots that seem bent on purging their own personal failures vicariously through their kids.

My wife and I are committed to keeping our children's world relatively free of conflict and confrontation. Soon enough life will introduce ample amounts of competition to them. Don't most Olympic champions and other sports amateurs avoid competing against **true** professionals without years of training and exposure to advanced competition?

It's *OK* to protect them and insulate them, exposing them through gradual exposure. They'll have a lifetime to experience the negative...prolong the positive for as long as possible. In so doing, they will be much better equipped to face problems when they finally do appear.

Prevention is better than cure.
—Desiderious Erasmus

What's the Solution?

So what is the answer? What can we do? Clearly, the *best* answer is for fathers to *be there.* The most influential dads are the ones that kids see when their eyes open in the morning and, again, as they close at night. These are dedicated fathers, fathers willing to skip an important board meeting to be at their son's first game. They earn their stripes by reacquainting themselves with the alphabet and long division so as to better explain it to their seven year old. These are dads that, even fatigued and stressed, still have time for a quick journey to Pooh Corner...

Fathers that come and get you, and drive you home, no questions asked, when you stayed out a little too late—annoyed but happy and relieved that you trusted him enough to keep you safe—*because he loves you.*

Fathers that throughout your lifetime remain as important and influential to you as the day you were born. Fathers so committed to their children that even when they've passed away, the power and influence of that bond—that commitment—still shapes the lives and character of their children and grandchildren.

Chronically absent fathers are indisputably becoming one of society's gravest ills. Only fathers who become redirected, devoted, and committed offer the best hope for a successful solution.

The concentration and dedication—the intangibles—are the deciding factors between who won and lost.

—Tom Seaver

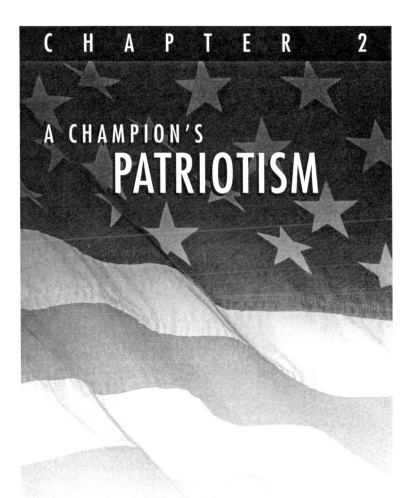

CHAPTER 2

A CHAMPION'S
PATRIOTISM

*Ask not what your country can do
for you, ask what you can do for
your country.*

John F. Kennedy

Champion Citizen, Champion Patriot!

It was the fourth of July and I was gazing fondly at my three-year-old son. In one hand, he waved a small American flag. In the other—damp and sticky from his snow cone—he proudly clutched a burning sparkler. It was a beautiful day, fireworks galore, in the company of family and friends, and my son's smile warmed my heart. Moments like this give me pause for thanks that I am a free citizen in the greatest nation on earth. But I am also aware of the immense sacrifices made by others for this freedom, as well as my obligation to honor and respect their legacy.

As parents, we have a moral obligation to instill in our children an understanding of American history and their respective role and obligation in maintaining and defending it. They must understand and appreciate the value of this freedom—and the costs associated with defending and maintaining it.

Today my son is merely waving a sparkly stick. Someday, he'll understand what that flag stands for. In a few years he will humble himself to the sacrifices endured to ensure his freedom. I'll teach him to live his life with the knowledge that he owes a huge debt that he may be called upon to someday repay.

Patriotism has its roots deep in the instincts and the affections. Love of country is the expansion of dutiful love.

—D. D. Field

Gone—But Not Forgotten

As the years accrue, the truly special moments we remember stand out. I often recall a special day in Hawaii as just such a seminal moment in the relationship with my own father.

It was December 7, 1991, and I had taken my 77-year-old father to Honolulu for the fiftieth anniversary of Japan's attack on Pearl Harbor. He was one of a select few Americans who understood and appreciated how that fateful day had changed America, and the world...forever.

Honolulu was bristling with somber remembrances and vivid World War II memorials—so richly deserved by the thinning ranks of veterans who actually fought in that war. I was deeply moved by their love of America and their pride in the freedom they fought for.

Later, Dad and I toured a mostly abandoned air base on the opposite side of the island where he had trained a half century ago. Suddenly fate intervened as he happened upon a fellow soldier he had served with in the Philippines. Unbelievably, his old comrade informed him that this very evening there was to be a reunion of my dad's old company that had fought together in World War II!

A nation which makes the final sacrifice for life and freedom does not get beaten.

—Kemal Ataturk

Being There...

That evening found me dining with two dozen men in their 60s, 70s, and 80s, who were reliving memories of the war. The festive mood succumbed quickly to tears and sadness—latent scars from the enormous human sacrifice that is necessary to keep America safe and its children free.

Slowly, one by one, each man stood up and recounted his own experiences and confronted his own memories. Most had witnessed friends blown up or had, themselves, been wounded. Most were still haunted by the knowledge that thousands of children had grown up fatherless—the ultimate cost of any war. No history class could have impressed upon me the gravity of that conflict, for clearly it was a horrible war that exacted a terrible price from those that served and fought it.

My awe and admiration of these aged warriors was suddenly interrupted when I realized that I was the only one in the room who had not experienced combat in World War II. Clearly, this was a very private and very personal meeting for these veterans. Sharing their war stories was an emotional experience that I'll never forget—a tremendous honor that I wasn't close to being worthy of.

Their stories brought tears to my eyes! They gave me a new lens with which to view my own father. The priceless gift that he and his comrades had fought for and died for became crystal clear. I know that I can never repay this debt, but I can honor it through my own actions and the lessons I teach my children.

*Never give in. Never, never, never, never!!
Never yield in any way great or small, except
to convictions of honor and good sense.
Never yield to force and the apparently
overwhelming might of the enemy!*
—Winston Churchill

The most inspirational moment of the evening occurred when someone casually asked, "Hey, was it all worth it?"

Perhaps for the first time, I fully understood why America would never be defeated by any force the world might throw at her.

Instantly, this room full of geriatrics, this scattered band of doddering gray-haired old men—this room full of grandfathers and great-grandfathers—responded like the soldiers they once were.

No words were spoken—none were needed. All I saw were the steel-eyed stares of strong, square-jawed soldiers, fists clenched, no fear, no doubt, ready for any threat or challenge to their country—their America! The question had been answered!

What is a society without a heroic dimension?
—Jean Baudrillard

Closer to Home . . .

Recent generations of Americans have lost touch with the human cost of preserving and protecting our freedom. 9/11 shook most of us out of any lingering apathy and violently reminded us what is real. Much like our national debt, quantifying our individual stake in freedom is difficult.

Let's bring it closer to home. You're out of town when a fire breaks out at your house where your wife and small children are sleeping...and trapped. When it's all over, your children and wife are safe. Sadly, a neighborhood father, who was your friend, with two kids of his own, was killed while saving your family. Watching his children grow up fatherless is the cost you bear for his heroics. How would you feel? What would you do? Wouldn't you spend every day—somehow—trying to repay this debt of honor?

Bear one another's burdens.

—The Holy Bible

To Whom Much Is Given, Much Is Expected

The freedom that is ours today is secured by a debt that can never be fully repaid. The best we can do is honor the memory and history of those who paid it for us. One of my life's purposes is to impress upon my kids how this great nation came to be and what might be expected of them to keep it that way. My children, your children, all of America's children need to be taught that *freedom isn't free*. Someday the bill collector may knock at *their* door.

Inevitably, our kids may be called upon to wear the uniform and serve in combat in defense of their nation. God forbid that day should come. If so, at least I'll have sent forth responsible and dedicated citizens who will understand why they're going and what's expected of them. The thought of my kids in harm's way is too excruciating to consider. But that pain is subordinate to our country's protection. Other fathers sent forth other sons and daughters with no less pain. Similarly my son and daughter will also go forth and serve if called. My hopes are reflected in the words of Thomas Paine, "Lord, if there must be trouble, let it be in my day, that my child may live in peace."

Every right implies a responsibility; Every opportunity, an obligation, Every possession, a duty.

—John D. Rockefeller

Aren't We All "Americans"?

Grave threats to America may also be festering within its own borders. Anti-American special interest groups are slowly dividing our traditional sense of purpose and unity. Their methods are the antithesis of traditional American culture; they seek to divide us not by honoring and respecting our historical "differences" but by *exploiting* them. Predictably this has eroded our national sense of unity and historical sense of cultural purpose. This practice of segmenting our citizens into groups with endless grievances and claims of victimization is tearing apart the fabric of our nation.

My heritage is Irish-Mexican-American but the only distinction worth claiming is American *citizen*. That's what I am, that's what you are, and it's who we all are! Everything else should be subordinated to the reality and responsibilities of that role. Period!

Because, you know what? If I'm in Bosnia or Vietnam, I'm fighting for America not Mexico or Ireland. In the foxholes of Normandy, the Mexican-American and African-American soldiers weren't thinking about Tijuana or Zimbabwe—they slugged their way through Europe and Asia to get home to Philadelphia and North Carolina! Hunkered down behind rocks in Korea or Guam, the Muslim- or Hindu-American soldiers dream only of returning to their loved ones in California and New York.

America has a distinct culture that has made us great. It is rooted in the concept of freedom and equality—constitutionally—for all of its citizens. The need for other distinctions does not exist except in the minds of those who prefer and practice "victimology" over responsible citizenship. From birth, we are all afforded identical constitutional rights and freedoms guaranteed by our founding fathers.

While the cultural fabric born of our historical melting pot is part and parcel of our nation's greatness, forcing these distinctions on others is becoming equally, and unnecessarily, divisive.

When we lose the right to be different,
we lose the privilege to be free!
—Charles Evans Hughes

The Founding Fathers—Real Sacrifice

My historical interests lie mostly in the twentieth century—World Wars I and II, in particular. These conflicts yielded stories of heroism and courage from America's "Greatest Generation." Until only recently, images of gray, powdered wigs worn by middle-age men at the Boston Tea Party, affixing collective signatures to lengthy documents, and making a concerted effort to antagonize the King of England, marked my knowledge of early American history.

Having children rekindled my interest in America's birth and early history. I, as all parents should, took the effort to really read and reacquaint myself with the Declaration of Independence and the Constitution to better understand their true and full meaning.

I was startled, and somewhat ashamed, at rediscovering the hardships and sacrifices our forefathers made to create this great nation. While America's entire history is marked by brave men doing battle under impossible conditions, *nothing* compares to the risks, dangers, and consequences endured by the original signers of the Declaration of Independence. It will forever stand as one of history's greatest acts of courage! Read on....

We all must hang together or most assuredly we shall hang separately.
—Benjamin Franklin

The King of England—America's Greatest Enemy?

Today our relationship with Great Britain is one of true partnership and commitment to common purpose, driven by a similar societal philosophy and moral beliefs. Since the vast majority of our country's population counts someplace in Europe as its point of origin, this relationship is natural—and desirable.

It was a different story for our ancestors. At the time our founding fathers were discussing and planning to break away from England as a colony to form a free and sovereign country—our ancestors faced horrific consequences. What they were planning was treason. A man caught *simply speaking out* against the throne could quite literally be hanged, his family imprisoned, his goods, property and belongings confiscated, and his name forever tarnished. England was quite unforgiving and harsh when dealing with colonists thought to be disloyal to England's king.

No child should be ignorant of his country's history and his inherent obligations and responsibilities. Defending America means knowing America and embracing *our* America. A true understanding of history also puts into proper context many of today's claims of perceived hardship.

*T*he most important thing in life is to live your life for something more important than your life.

—Anonymous

America's First Heroes . . . the Men Who Risked It All!

Of the 56 original signers to the Declaration of Independence, nine died of wounds or other wartime hardships. Five were captured and imprisoned, in each case with exceptionally brutal treatment. Several lost wives, sons or entire families. One lost all thirteen of his children. Two wives were brutally savaged. All were at one time or another victims of manhunts and driven from their homes. Twelve signers had their homes completely burned. Seventeen lost everything they owned. *Yet not one, not a single one, defected or went back on his pledged word!* Their honor, and the nation they sacrificed so much to create, is still intact. At the very least, their sacrifice should mandate knowledge and appreciation of it from all American citizens who have benefited from it.

*A*s soon as sacrifice becomes a duty
and necessity to mankind,
I see no limit to the horizon,
which opens before him

—Ernest Renan

The Ultimate Sacrifice . . . What Would You Have Done?

Could any among us do it today?...

And, finally, there is the story of New Jersey signer, Abraham Clark.

He gave his only two sons to the officer corps in the Revolutionary Army. They were captured and sent to that infamous British prison hulk afloat in New York harbor know as the Hell Ship "Jersey," where *11,000 American captives were to die.* The younger Clarks were treated with a special brutality because of who their father was. One was put in solitary confinement and given no food.

With the end almost in sight and the war nearly won, no one could have blamed Abraham Clark for acceding to the British request when they offered him his sons' lives if he would recant and come out for the king and parliament. The utter despair in this man's heart, the anguish in his very soul, must reach out to each one of us down through 200 years with his answer: *"No."*

The 56 signers of the Declaration of Independence proved by their every deed that they made no idle boast when they composed the most magnificent curtain line in history—

And for the support of this Declaration with a firm reliance on the protection of divine providence, we mutually pledge to each other our lives, our fortunes, and our sacred honor.

* * *

Our history is clear, our heritage safe, our freedoms guaranteed, and our nation is still in its infancy on the world stage. Truly, the best still lies before us. Do your part to guarantee it. Educate your children, America's children, on how it got that way and what's required of them to keep it that way. Raise them to understand that as American citizens they have an enormous responsibility. My kids will know and understand that their civic obligations are not a burden or inconvenience … but a very real and great honor.

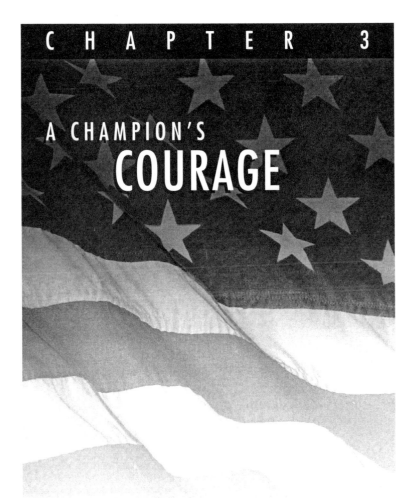

CHAPTER 3

A CHAMPION'S
COURAGE

*Courage is the first of human
qualities because it is the quality
which guarantees all others.*

Winston Churchill

"Real" Courage

My son was barely two when he taught me a lesson in real courage that I would never forget. He personified the preceding quotation.

Braden is a sweet and unassuming little guy who generally avoids conflict and confrontation. He hasn't a mean bone in his body and doesn't remotely understand the concept of teasing or bullying. He has a natural respect for all people and is happiest when others around him are happy.

I had arrived early at his preschool one day and stood back watching his natural interaction with his classmates. Braden was unaware of my arrival. He was sitting at a table with five or six other little boys and girls who were all having their snack of punch and cookies.

I saw his reaction to an incident that clearly disturbed him. The older boy next to him took the drink away from the little girl sitting across the table when she wasn't looking and replaced hers with his empty glass.

Unaware of Dad's presence, Braden was on his own. I could see from his expression that he was puzzled and disturbed by what he saw. Suddenly the little guy reached out and switched the glasses to their original positions!

Tears welled up in my eyes. I had just witnessed the essence of courage and integrity from a little boy. Barely old enough to talk, my son had just established his ability to discern right from wrong and had demonstrated the needed courage to act upon it. I knew then that the seeds of character had taken root. Courage and integrity would always be personal traits unique to Braden's makeup and personality—a priceless gift he'll pass along to his kids some day. Parents concerned about their children's future should remember that the mightiest oak was once a tiny seedling.

Far better it is to dare mighty things, to win glorious triumphs even though checkered by failures, than to rank with those poor spirits who neither enjoy much nor suffer much because they live in the gray twilight that knows not victory or defeat.

—Teddy Roosevelt

How Do You Define Courage?

To me, courage isn't the absence of fear but the strength of character to manage it. Courage stems from an inner confidence, born of gentleness—nurtured by love, practiced quietly.

Our individual capacity for courage is linked closely to our level of confidence when facing danger or uncertainty. Your own moral compass will also be your child's. The quality of this compass will determine the capacity for courage in both of you. It's that simple.

When your moral compass finds its true north—
courage will naturally follow.

*All of life's significant battles are waged
within ourselves.*

—Sheldon Kopp

Courage to Do the Right Thing at the Right Time

Winning or losing, success or failure, even life and death, can swing in the balance of a single moment of decision—or indecision—on events in our lives. One dumb mistake, a single poor choice, a moment of fatal hesitation, can mean the difference between the best and the most tragic outcomes. A lack of courage stemming from every adolescent's desire to be liked and included often spells disaster for the weak and insecure.

It's an accepted truism that drilling and repetitious exercises in key skill areas improves everyone's prospects for success and outstanding performance. Indeed, *practice does make perfect.*

Two great examples come to mind. The training required of the men and women in America's armed forces and the coaching philosophy of the legendary UCLA basketball coach John Wooden.

Confidence and courage come through preparation and practice.

—Source Unknown

I had the rare privilege of visiting Coach Wooden at his home in California. In my humble opinion, John Wooden is the most decent gentleman I have ever met—or will likely ever meet. He personifies my belief that life is simple when guided by one's conviction, sense of purpose, and an unrelenting faith in God.

In college basketball most coaches rely on the use of "scouts" to attend the games of opposing teams. The theory goes that by sneaking around your enemy's camp you'll discover some hidden "weakness" that your team can exploit. Sounds reasonable. Weasel-like spies have been utilized since the dawn of man.

In stark contrast to his contemporaries, Coach Wooden had no use for this practice. He believed in drilling his own teams to their maximum levels of capability and performance and then, in his words, "I'd rather let the other fella worry about how to stop us." As Bill Walton, former UCLA All-American, remembers, "Coach Wooden had us at such a high level of practiced proficiency that once the games began they seemed like slow motion because we didn't think—we simply reacted...."

In the military the stakes are much higher but the philosophy is the same. Through repetitious drilling, soldiers practice until their response to dangerous situations becomes one of cool reaction—not fatal hesitation. Confidence is courage's foundation and confidence is gained through mastery of our pursuits.

Guess what? We can use this on our youngsters. I take every opportunity to *drill* my kids when learning situations present themselves. Most parents preach the "what." Put your helmet on, look both ways in traffic, avoid strangers. Of greater importance to their futures is the "why" inherent in these lessons. "Because I said so" is banter from the past. Explaining why provides greater safeguards for their future.

Through practice and repetition, their thoughtful responses—in all things important—will become instant reactions. The eventual difference may amount to only seconds but lost lives may have been saved had those seconds been available to children less fortunate.

They didn't choose tragedy...tragedy chose them.
—Juliett Binoche

The Courage to Accept, and Live With, Tragedy

The height of courage is the acceptance of devastating consequences born of random, freakish fate. A special brand of courage is required to accept and live with this type of personal tragedy. No person better exemplifies this trait than Mike Utley. He is the epitome of the American warrior and he should be an example to all of us faced with daunting personal tragedies.

Mike Utley's entire life was football—culminating in an All-Pro career with the Detroit Lions. On a single freak play Mike's neck was broken. I can't begin to comprehend the loss of being an NFL lineman one second to being permanently paralyzed in less time than it takes to snap your fingers. From that point on—Mike was paralyzed from the waist down, forever confined to a wheelchair. Faced with this seismic loss, few of us would recover, let alone thrive and prosper. But few of us are Mike Utley.

I met Mike at the gym where I worked out. It was impossible not to notice this massive athletic man—in a wheelchair, throwing around barbells like a madman! We soon became friends and I saw firsthand his amazing will power and determination to walk again.

I have made a personal commitment to not look back, but rather forward, to all of the opportunities I have that lie ahead.

—Mike Utley

A Profile in Courage

The pursuit of excellence has no boundaries except those we place on ourselves. With football gone, Mike became proficient at skiing, sky diving, scuba diving, speed boat racing, and basketball—things frightening to many of us with *no* physical limitations. Mike shared with me his newfound purpose, *"The only fear I have is the fear of not doing the things I want to do before I die. Fear is something you put in front of yourself. It is man-made, man-concocted. I deal with fear but I'm not afraid."*

On February 15, 1999, with the aid of some close friends, Mike Utley rose from his wheel chair and took those precious few steps that no one believed possible just a few short years ago. Mike recalls, "Soon after my injury, a doctor came into my room and told my mom, dad, and my agent that I would never walk again. I immediately told that doctor, "Get the hell out of my room!" I also told him he had no right telling me or anyone else that they can't do something, only God has that right—and he wasn't talking."

My admiration and respect for Mike Utley is beyond words. I have no doubt that his determination, will power, and love of life will enable him to defeat this opponent as he has others.

In a different way, Mike Utley is as formidable as he ever was doing battle in the NFL. I'm convinced his best has yet to be seen. My sincere thanks to him and I wish him God's speed.

Confidence is courage at ease.
—Daniel Maher

Courage to Face Down and Resist Their Peers

Defaulting to peer pressure in years past may have resulted in toilet-papering the principal's house, sneaking a kiss at recess, or smoking a cigarette in a friend's basement. Today the threats and consequences are much more serious and potentially lethal.

To a young person, peer pressure is the single greatest challenge he or she will face on the path to adulthood. Courage commands a premium in the company of our peers and is the only protection available against ignorance and stupidity.

Most tragic incidents spring from bad judgment and poor decision-making in an attempt to "impress" those around them. For children and young adults, legitimate self-confidence engenders courage, which trumps peer pressure every time. It's a parent's job to build their self-confidence when they're young. It takes a lot of courage to stand up to people you most want respect and acceptance from.

Courage is a special kind of knowledge: the knowledge of how to fear what ought to be feared and how not to fear what ought not to be feared.

—David Ben-Gurion

Courage to Fear What Ought to Be Feared

On the surface this seems so simple as to be silly. Don't walk around outside in a lightning storm, barefoot, holding a nine-iron over your head. Don't try and breathe underwater without scuba gear. Don't tease an angry dog...and stay away from too much cheese.

If you think this is so obvious, simply recall your own reckless abandon and remember that with youth comes heightened feelings of invincibility and immortality. *Tempting fate* is a national pastime among young adults. Movies glamorize the "reckless and fearless" leading characters in their films. The most popular TV shows involve "extreme sports" where fame and entertainment value increase with the degree of risk one is willing to take. Don't assume your kids have a healthy fear or respect of things dangerous...*you* didn't.

Respect and self-respect are covered in another chapter but they go hand in hand and are often the flip side of the same coin. While teaching your kids what to fear...make sure you also point out what to respect.

You don't drown by falling in the water; you drown by staying there.

—Edwin Louis Cole

The Courage to Fail—and Get Back Up!

Failure isn't a noble pursuit but it's certainly nothing to fear. I've never cared for the negative connotation that normally accompanies the word. I prefer Thomas Edison's view of "failure." Edison was unsuccessful in thousands of attempts to invent the light bulb. He scoffed at any suggestion of failure. To the contrary, Edison merely believed he was successful in identifying ways that the light bulb could *not* be created. Like many of history's pioneers Edison was blazing new trails that required taking chances with the unknown.

Throughout our lifetime "the unknown" will continually challenge us to discover our physical, emotional, and intellectual boundaries and limitations. The failures in my life have been profound and numerous. And yet what success I've known is attributable more to my losses than to my wins.

John Wooden, former UCLA basketball coach, believes that there is no such thing as failure if you've done your best to prepare for something and then fall short. There's no shame or dishonor in that.

I personally never use the word *failure* because I don't enjoy inviting *negativity* into my life. I would recommend that the word be stricken from everyone's dialogue—especially the use of it around impressionable children.

Failure should be our teacher, not our undertaker. Failure is delay, not defeat. It is

a temporary detour, not a dead end. Failure
is something we can avoid only by saying
nothing, doing nothing, and being nothing.

—Denis Waitley

The Courage to Succeed When Negative Influences Conspire to Destroy Your Dreams

Louis Pasteur, Albert Einstein, Jonas Salk, Thomas Edison, Henry Ford—all names we commonly associate with America's greatest thinkers, inventors, and innovators. What obstacle did they all have in common, something they all had to overcome? To a man, they were universally criticized, routinely ridiculed, frequently impugned, always doubted, and regularly vilified as nuts and quacks. And don't forget that we're just a few hundred years removed from executing people who claimed the world was round...

The characteristics that distinguished these creative geniuses and giants were *courage*—and *persistence*. They all had the courage to explore uncharted waters and the persistence to stay the course, even in the face of the ridicule and scrutiny of idiots.

Fear is met and destroyed with courage.

—James F. Bell

The Courage to Confront Fear

The strength and courage needed to confront the unknown also comes from individual confidence. That's why it's so important to do things that let your children experience what success feels like. Otherwise most children will simply be content to grow up sitting in the shade of their parent's trees.

A test of what is real is that it is hard and rough. Joys are found in it, not pleasure. What is pleasant belongs to dreams.

—Simone Weil

The Courage to Accept Reality

As much as we wish it were different, life is not easy—it is, in fact, quite hard and demanding. Many people think that fairness should be the standard—but life is not fair, it's often unjust. Too often the best man loses or dies and less deserving people always seem to get ahead. Evil is rewarded, virtue is penalized. Thrift is discouraged, excess is celebrated. Honesty is impugned, dishonesty is casually shrugged off.

* * *

Every day I want my kids to walk out the front door confident in their ability to deal with *what is* and the courage to create their own *what will be*. It is every father's responsibility to build his children's confidence and courage—which can only strengthen and enhance their character and integrity.

No matter what choices our kids make there will always be someone telling them, *"You are wrong—you can't do it."* It's these moments when all your work and dedication will pay off as they stand up straight, look those people in the eye, and confidently walk away—thankful you gave them "idiot insurance." Any temptation to give credence to their critics will have courage as an ally. Temptation rarely gets past courage.

The dangers our kids face are probably going to get worse before they get better. In the meantime, fathers need to set the standard for courage, integrity, and bravery. As Winston Churchill aptly declared, "Courage is the first of human qualities because it is the quality that guarantees all the others."

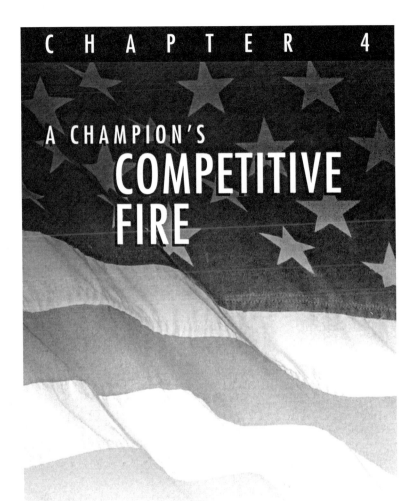

CHAPTER 4

A CHAMPION'S COMPETITIVE FIRE

The only way to be number one...
is to be number one.

Unknown

Life Is the Personification of Competition

Two young boys are walking home from school when, for no particular reason, the pace begins to quicken—as does their pulse! Though lifelong buddies, they quickly weigh each other's mettle!

The pace accelerates, now just short of a trot, as each boy smiles inwardly in eager anticipation of the imminent contest. Suddenly, they break into a spontaneous gallop! The race is on....!

Isn't competition the very essence of our existence? Isn't it what drives most of us to excel and achieve? Don't most of us at least dream of the view from the mountaintop? If so—doesn't it make sense to teach our children how to compete and how to win?

Competition is what we live for—it is the circulatory system of the human race. Like it or not most of us are subject to some degree of competitive influence. Our success and happiness, if not our survival, often hinge upon our ability to compete effectively.

Character cannot be developed in ease and quiet. Only through experiences of trial and suffering can the soul be strengthened, vision cleared, ambition inspired and success achieved.

—Helen Keller

Competition Is Healthy—For Everyone

Life is little more than uninterrupted competition. Opponents dot our horizons from dawn to dusk—cradle to grave. Even the most ardent anti-competition advocates grudgingly acknowledge that competition permeates nearly all aspects of American life. Dads— do your kids a big favor. Prepare them to confront and relish the competition in their lives.

I've often wondered how Helen Keller would have coped in today's world. Had she been born blind and deaf in today's America, she would likely be knee-deep in food stamps, inundated with government programs, and standing in welfare lines. She would want for nothing...*except her independence and dignity!*

In Helen Keller's own words, "The marvelous richness of human experience would lose something of rewarding joy if there were no limitations to overcome. The hilltop hour would not be half so wonderful if there were no dark valleys to traverse."

Helen Keller was a true warrior and an American hero! With only determination and some assistance from a dedicated teacher, she conquered her disability, graduated from Radcliffe College and became a tremendously successful and *independent* contributor to society.

Today, the self-appointed stewards of America's handicapped citizens are sending the message that people with handicaps or disabilities can't succeed on their own without special programs, accommodations, and government assistance.

The mere fact that you have obstacles to overcome is in your favor...

—Robert Collier

What Exactly Is "Competition"?

Competition presents us with that rare opportunity to measure our personal or professional progress in our respective fields and endeavors. It is normally associated with athletic contests, yet this represents but a fraction of the unending challenges that routinely confront most of us. We all engage in uniquely personal kinds of competition. Contests specific to our own dreams and expectations.

As a 46-year-old father my own definition of "competition" has changed. I now see that the true measure of *competitive spirit* lies more in our ability to overcome life's unending obstacles. Keeping my kids away from drugs means more than slamming the winning home run. Crafting their character means far more than shaping my own resume.

Probably the happiest period in life most frequently is in middle age, when the eager passions of youth are cooled, and the infirmities of age not yet begun; as we see that the shadows, which are at morning and evening so large, almost entirely disappear at midday.

—Thomas Arnold

47

Competitive Spirit Determines Our "True" Age

When I was young, only being first to cross the finish line fanned the flames of my competitive spirit. My tools, then, were my muscles and athletic skills, and my workshop—the weight room and competitive arenas. Life was simple. Success was determined by the margin of victory.

But as the years passed, my competitive fires were drawn more to professional endeavors. Success was measured by the size of the deal and the style in which it was completed. I still competed athletically—but age began benchmarking my sports accomplishments. I accepted that my brain would outlast my brawn and adjusted my life accordingly. The tools I brandished were intellect and exceptional communication skills. The arenas morphed into college classrooms, customer boardrooms, and my computer's hard drive. It was the 1980s and I had embraced that generation's mantra, *"Whoever dies with the most stuff...wins."*

I'm heading for 50 and my athletic victories are behind me. So is the notion that material possessions mean anything beyond useful utility. My competitive energies are focused on new and equally challenging opponents, no less formidable than those of the past.

Be ready when opportunity comes. Luck occurs when preparation & opportunity meet.

—Roy D. Chapin Jr.

Be Prepared When Chance Smiles

Successful people don't just work hard and hope for the best. Great leaders *anticipate* long before opportunity presents itself. More often than not, opportunity *never* presents itself. Many people prepare for greatness. Few get the chance to demon-strate it.

Spectacular achievement is always preceded by spectacular preparation.

—Robert Schuler

Dick Kovacevich—America's Best Banker?

"Focus on the opportunity rather than the problem," was the message from Richard M. Kovacevich, CEO of Wells Fargo. No finer words better encapsulate his personal or professional mantra and no company has better promoted the vision of its leader.

History will distinguish Dick Kovacevich as a visionary who was uniquely special and ideally suited for the demanding challenges facing him in the high-stakes banking industry. Breaking with tradition and his competitors, he consistently assigned equal importance to customers, employees, and shareholders alike. Early on, he recognized and understood that quantum leap changes were simply unattainable without the inclusion, trust, and commitment of his employees. He was right! The success and standards of excellence that embody today's Wells Fargo exemplify the characteristics of a true *American Champion* that this book seeks to honor and promote.

One-half of knowing what you want is in knowing what you must give up before you get it.

—Sidney Howard

Dick Kovacevich was serious. Equally important ...he was prepared. Rather than pursue a promising career in professional baseball, he decided to accept an athletic scholarship from Stanford University, where he graduated with a business degree. It was the first, of many, timely and fortuitous decisions he would make. As a baseball player, he was talented but no "sure thing" to make the big leagues. His decision was validated when he tore up his shoulder in a college baseball game. Baseball was gone...but he exited with a degree from Stanford University in his back pocket.

When I was a young man I observed that nine out of ten things I did were failures. I didn't want to be a failure, so I did ten times more work.

—George Bernard Shaw

As a young man, Dick Kovacevich wasn't going to gamble his future on "faith." He knew hard work was his only ticket to the *major leagues* of the business world. Dick's wife, Mary Jo, remembers, "Dick has always set very high standards for himself and has always worked extremely hard to achieve success. He strongly believes that he isn't any different from other people and that hard work was the only way for him to distinguish himself."

Without failure we never learn our limitations and, thus, are denied the knowledge of what we are truly capable of and what we can truly be.

—Dick Kovacevich

Competition—Business Style

Dick Kovacevich reaffirms the role of competition in all facets of life: "Sports and competition were always an extremely important influence on my life. Not just as a way to make money or get a college scholarship, but also on my style of management in terms of motivation and teamwork, of setting high goals at home and at work, and in learning to interact with people who may have diversely different qualities and backgrounds."

Sports don't build character— they reveal it.

—John Wooden

Mother Nature

Mother Nature trumps everything and she will normally have her way with all of us. Success is partially defined by how long we can keep her at bay.

Two years ago I had a mild heart attack. Avoiding a second one is a crucial challenge. It presents an unusual problem— balancing my aggressive nature while avoiding obvious risks to my health. Victory's reward will be the number of years I have to educate and treasure my children.

The past cannot be changed. The future is yet in your power.

—Mary Pickford

Protecting My Children

A famous college football coach, having just completed an undefeated season, was asked, *"Hey coach, is this your greatest team ever?"* The coach shrugged his shoulders and replied, *"I won't know for twenty or thirty years."*

His message—their football victories were immaterial measured against their adult contributions. Fathers, like coaches, can't fully substantiate, in the short term, the lessons they teach.

This is where today's fathers drop the ball. Many kids reach adulthood without being **raised.** My own are three and five. I believe that the only accurate and meaningful measure of my value as a father are the minutes I invest interacting with my children. As described above, the final score may be years away but that day will surely come. The day when their character and judgment are all that separate them from the dangers and negative influences stalking all children. We insure our most valuable assets. The minutes invested with your kids insures the only asset that counts.

Tragic outcomes can usually be traced to small but vital factors. A careless electrician cuts corners and, years later, the house burns down—killing an entire family. The minutia matters. Small things count. The insignificant...isn't. So invest the time and enjoy the comfort and satisfaction of a job well done.

Success is the sum of small efforts, repeated day in and day out...

—Robert Collier

Success Defined

John Wooden is arguably the finest and most influential coach in the history of college basketball. His definition of success is simple and accurate. *"Success is attained when someone does his absolute best to prepare himself to perform at the highest level he is capable of."* If you've done your best—nothing more should be expected and acceptance of the outcome will provide lessons for future efforts. There's a sublime beauty to this rationale. It removes your opponents and obstacles from the equation. It is the pinnacle of empowerment! Responsibility lies squarely in the lap of the one person qualified to make it happen—each of us, individually. The irony is the likelihood that our most formidable opponent will be ourselves.

You must keep your mind on the objective Not on the obstacle.

—William Randolph Hearst

Keep Your Eye on the Ball

What does the above quote have to do with competition? For starters, America's culture has evolved into one focused more on the obstacles than the finish line. We're more obsessed with *why* he failed than with *how could we help him succeed?* Our culture is becoming more inclined to excuse and explain away unacceptable behavior than firmly confront, discipline, and punish it.

I'm appalled by ongoing efforts to ban or *"scale down"* competition for younger school kids. Many failing educators, unable to compete or properly educate our children, are sanitizing and manipulating test scores and grades! Rather than confront and solve the problems they seek only to mask actual performance and achievement. They seek to replace historical ideals of *"Being the best"* with *"Oh well, we all did OK."*

The same misguided principles are being applied to sports. Middle schools across the nation have all but eliminated competitive sports, replacing them with recreational or intramural "activities." Their emphasis is on *participation—not competition.*

You can learn a <u>line</u> from a win and a <u>book</u> from a defeat.

—Paul Brown

"Let 'Em Play!"

Give me a break! Can you see such kids negotiating a raise with their future boss? "Well, Johnny, you didn't actually improve much and your contributions were obscure to the point of anonymity. But I'm going to give you a 15 percent raise just for participating and playing nicely with your peers!" Do these people truly believe this is a responsible and effective way to provide the skills these kids will need in the future?

Recently a youth soccer league, with players ranging in age from 5 to 15, banned *scoring* from their games. The kids play for a while and go home, presumably satisfied just to "participate." (Does anyone believe these kids don't know who actually won?)

A recent Texas high school valedictorian was denied the opportunity to speak at her graduation. School administrators felt that by recognizing her, underachievers and nonachievers might feel *bad*. Did they ever consider that these underachievers might be inspired and motivated by her achievements? Might they be stirred to reach higher? That makes too much sense—better to yank down the star than encourage others to reach skyward.

Worse, cheating is going on around the country. Inner-city school officials have manipulated test data to cloak the actual results. When the revelations became public they justified their actions in the belief that the kids weren't capable of passing *without* assistance—cheating.

This reasoning must have been particularly uplifting for the students who actually put forth the time and effort to pass these tests unassisted. By association, *their* test results are now suspect. No one wins a fixed contest. The end result is a larger pool of losers.

*You cannot strengthen the weak
by weakening the strong.*

—Ronald Reagan

Quit Dumbing Them Down

Lifting performance from the bottom is the only way to encourage performance improvement. Pulling it down from the top only weakens the entire structure and benefits no one. Incentivize—don't penalize. Reward effort—punish sloth. Failure to exercise sensibility may have future generations of school children taking pride in T-shirts blaring such inspirational messages as:

"Mediocrity is COOL!"

"The tower? What's wrong with the basement?"

"Why fly when you can walk?"

"Yeeeaaah! We're number 37! We're number 37!"

"I'll do it tomorrow—maybe."

"I got a 95? I'm sorry! I'll study less and improve."

"I'm sorry I beat you—can you ever forgive me?"

"Winning is for losers."

This silliness is anathema to the history and ideals of America. It also explains who is behind our declining intelligence scores and diminishing work ethic. Should anyone be surprised by the decline in the confidence and trust we have in our public schools?

The _ultimate_ victory in competition is derived from the inner satisfaction of knowing that you have done your best and that you have gotten the most out of what you had to give.

—Howard Cosell

Encourage Them to Compete

Our best memories are usually associated with our most difficult challenges and contests. The times we ran until our lungs almost burst! Studying until we fell asleep by the moonlight? Imaginations consumed with beating opponents both real and imagined? Wasn't _any_ ribbon or medal placed around your neck among your most cherished memories and possessions? Doesn't winning feel better than losing? Well...doesn't it?

Encourage competition in your children! Why? Because life is an increasingly difficult and intense struggle. Unfair as it may seem—life has winners and life has losers. _**It always has and it always will.**_ The lessons are clear and at times harsh, but when you work harder and longer, you perform better.

Lazy slackers should be embarrassed. The sooner the better! Sparing children the humiliation that accompanies defeat or failure denies them the best opportunities for positive change.

Too many parents seem determined to remedy their own failings at their children's expense. If their kids avoid the same mistakes and predicaments it somehow wipes _their_ slate clean. It actually has the opposite effect—that of _transference._ They transfer their own anxieties and insecurities—and eventually their problems, onto the shoulders of their children. Let them blaze their own trails! You had your chance. Allow them theirs.

Life's challenges are not supposed to paralyze you, they're supposed to help you discover who you are.
—Bernice Johnson Reagon

It's Been Tried Before—It Still Doesn't Work

There's a term for efforts to "equalize" society. It's called socialism or communism and it has been an abject failure anywhere it was embraced. It failed because you cannot manage or reconcile basic human nature. Why? For it to work, each individual must subordinate himself to the *"greater good."* What is lost attempting to equalize the output of non-equal people is quality and initiative.

With no clear winners or losers, no rewards or consequences, why expend the effort? Few people are naturally inclined to excel without the prospect of recognition or reward. With no distinction of first from last—why dedicate and practice? Go home, eat chips, come in last, and receive the same rewards. One look at post-communist Russia or East Germany answers that question. A competitive America is basking in historical economic growth and prosperity while post-communist nations can barely feed their citizens or contain corruption of leaders and public officials.

To be tested is good. The challenged life may be the best therapist.

59

—Gail Sheehy

Vote YES for Competition

Competition is the limestone across which we draw our blades. It is our very lifeblood.

Competition has also been the catalyst of nearly every great historical achievement or discovery. Gil Atkinson aptly declares, "Thank God for competition! When our competitors upset our plans or outdo our designs, they open the infinite possibilities of our own work to us."

W. D. Toland, "Competition as the 'life' of trade surely is a tremendous spur to progress. Is it not the pursued man or business that advances through persistent effort to keep ahead? The constant striving to maintain leadership ever involves new ways and means of accomplishing more efficiently and thus it is that the 'pursued is the progressive man.' Put your pursuers on the payroll...."

*There is nothing that fear and hope
does not allow men to do.*

—Marquis De Vauvenargues

Strongly Discourage "Quitting"

There may be rare occasions where unusual circumstances justify quitting. It is, as it should be, a decision motivated by personal circumstances.

However, especially with younger children, quitting can become habit-forming, providing an *easy out* when things in their life get tough. Too often, *"I can't do this"* means, *"I don't want to do this"* or *"I am unwilling to work to get this done."* Be firm. Don't let your kids off the hook unless you honestly believe they have a legitimate reason to abandon efforts toward a personal goal or objective.

I know people who ran from fights simply out of fear. Frequently, they were the same kids who'd become at ease with quitting. As adults, predictably, they've become troubled and insecure—always haunted, always looking over their shoulder, always second-guessing themselves. Their mantra, *"What if I had just..."* was all too familiar. What could be a worse nickname for a young boy or girl than *quitter?*

Dads? Instead of giving your kids a pass...give them the following poem to keep their heads high and their eyes looking forward.

DON'T QUIT!

When things go wrong, as they sometimes will,
When the road you're trudging seems all uphill,
When the funds are low and the debts are high,
And you want to smile, but you have to sigh,
When care is pressing you down a bit —
Rest if you must, but don't you quit!

Life is queer with its twists and turns,
And every one of us sometimes learns,

61

And many a person turns about
When they might have won had they stuck it out.
Don't give up though the pace seems slow—
You may succeed with just one more blow.
Often the struggler has given up
When he might have captured the victor's cup;
And he learned too late, when the night came down,
How close he was to the golden crown.

Success is failure turned inside out—
So stick to the fight when you're hardest hit—
It's when things seem worst that you mustn't quit.

Our Heart May Sustain Us But Competition Inspires Us

Life has more losers than winners. Teach kids to accept both with an equal measure of pride, dignity, respect, and humility. Pursuing excellence is worthy and noble. Losing after giving their best effort is no different.

CHAPTER 5

A CHAMPION'S
KINDNESS

*Kindness is more than deeds.
It is an attitude, an expression,
a look, a touch. It is anything
that lifts another person.*

C. Neil Strait

America's Kindness—Our Gift to the World

America's kindness has always anchored America's strength. The fact that we have emerged as the world's lone superpower is no coincidence nor difficult to explain. Our power is derived from our judgment in projecting it, usually on behalf of the oppressed, the impoverished, or the downtrodden. America will always have its critics but when historical danger yet again threatens the world, only America will be entrusted with the task of "making things right." It is because only America possesses, and has demonstrated, the moral clarity and cultural integrity to take on such an enormous responsibility. More American blood has been shed from heroic acts of compassion and kindness than malevolence. Kind and gentle children are generally strong and compassionate. It's a trait worth instilling and relishing.

One should distinguish between charity and kindness. Kindness costs nothing to give yet is treasured to receive. Our capacity for kindness will define our true character and determine the amount of *real* happiness we will enjoy.

There's no accurate means of measuring how many kids we've lost to prisons, drugs, and violence who might have been salvaged had they experienced a little kindness when they were young. Nor do we know how many troubled youths *did* make it through because someone cared enough to stop, look, listen, and try to understand. Common sense and compassion demand we err on the latter side.

Our strength can be measured by our kindness. Kindness is the golden chain by which society is bound together.
—Johanne Wolfgang Von Goethe

Kindness Repels Violence

When it rains we don rubbers and ponchos. To lose weight we consume less, not more, calories. Levity and laughter is prescribed for unhappiness and despair. Thirst is quenched with water and tension through relaxation. Doesn't it stand to reason that kindness might gradually inoculate us from violence? Kindness is so easy and painless to administer yet so powerful and effective, and yet too many children continue to slide into the abyss. Why? Is the remedy wrong or aren't enough people practicing it?

I feel the capacity to care is the single thing That gives life its deepest significance.
—Pablo Casals

In America? A Chilling Reality

Last year over 29 million youths committed at least one act of violence against a sibling or family member. *TWENTY-NINE MILLION!*

Research has confirmed that the violent behaviors of an eight year old, *if no intervention occurs*, will predict perfectly their same behaviors at age 38.

Other studies show that over 80 percent of all children entering kindergarten feel good about themselves. By fifth grade, that percentage has dropped to 20 percent and by twelfth grade it is only 5 percent. Think about that! Out of 1,000 hopeful and happy five-year-old kindergartners a full 950 will have had their self-esteem shattered by their senior year in high school. What is causing this and, more urgently, what, if anything, is being done about it?

The root cause is day-to-day peer aggression. It takes many forms but the most egregious are peer "put-downs" and "bullying." Such tactics gradually diminish *anyone's* sense of worth. Sadly, in today's world, a kindness *oasis* is hard to come by.

Bullies are always cowards at heart and may be credited with a pretty safe instinct in scenting their prey.
—Anna Julia Cooper

Ending the Bully's Reign

A report was released recently suggesting that Columbine High School and its administrators tolerated a pervasive culture of "bullying," particularly by its athletes. It was also suggested that this culture could have been a mitigating factor in motivating Eric Harris and Dylan Klebold to murderous action.

These rumors have been circulating since the day of the killings. I never gave them much thought nor did I feel that it was likely that any sort of bullying could have contributed to the deranged behavior of these two rabid animals. For the most part, I still don't.

Most of us attended schools inhabited by bullies. Unpleasant as it was, it was a normal component of our adolescent landscape. Dealing with it challenged all of us to come up with a solution based on our individual circumstances. In a far less onerous environment, is it so much different than confronting and defeating America's enemies during times of war?

Be that as it may...I've changed my mind. Not because I think bullying motivates its victims into acts of violent crimes. Nor do I believe that it permanently damages the lives of the bullied or accept that conflict and confrontation are necessarily wrong or bad.

My mind changed because my heart changed. Bullying is simply wrong. We are all better than that—or at least should be. Our kids need to be more compassionate and empathetic. Kindness and respect are in short supply these days and any one of us can make a difference if we choose to. School is a valuable and important rite of passage. No child should fear attending for fear of being targeted by idiots!

When I was in eighth grade I used to tease and torment a fellow student named Calvin. To me it was all innocent and amusing. I never paused to view it from Calvin's shoes.

Calvin was your classic geek. Straight A's, three feet tall with a sad mop of unkempt hair, he viewed life through Coke-bottle-thick glasses, struggling daily to carry his load of books. I never physically hurt Calvin, but I came to understand how badly I embarrassed and intimidated him.

Our "seminal" moment erupted one day in the locker room after gym class. I had parked myself behind Calvin, flicking his ears as he tried to dress— an indignity Calvin routinely tolerated. But today was different. Today, Calvin wheeled around and punched me right in the nose!

With my nose swelling, my pride dented, and my temper near eruption—I glared down at Calvin. He was standing in front of me—terrified and shaking. Such moments tend to shape our souls and I found myself speaking out, "Good shot, Calvin!" I massaged my swollen nose...and walked away.

I'll never be certain whose life changed more that day. Mine, in the realization that one man's teasing is torture to another. Or Calvin's, trembling with fear, desperately trying to gather the courage to confront his worst fears. One thing is certain. On that fateful day Calvin *recovered* his pride and dignity while I *discovered* my compassion and humility.

We'll never know, with certainty, what inspired Harris and Klebold to Columbine's madness and carnage. Personally, it's my belief that some extremely bad apples are occasionally visited upon us to remind society of evil's existence. Attempting to attribute it to anything else is pointless and perhaps reckless.

What we can do is use the tragedy to encourage people to treat each other better—reminded that life is fragile and occasionally very short. Being kind and gentle is truly life's best measure of a man's strength.

The flower of kindness will grow. Maybe not now, but it will someday. And in kind that kindness will flow, for kindness grows in this way.
—Robert Alan

A Man to Remember, Joe Dumars, Jr.

Kindness *can* change the world, one child at a time. . .

I never had the privilege of meeting Joe Dumars Jr.; he died before I began writing this book. However, his wife, Ophelia, and some of his children shared his story with me. Through them, he has become a powerful force in my life—and the lives of my kids—by the immense and powerful legacy he left behind. This story is a belated tribute to a man of enormous character, kindness, and decency. If in his absence, his life can have this kind of positive impact on someone like me—I can only envision the positive influence he must have had on those fortunate enough to stumble upon his path in person. It seems only natural and fitting that a man who influenced so many lives should continue to do so through the splendid example and influence he left behind. He is proof positive that regardless of your station in life you can have a positive impact on any child you encounter— if only you desire to do so.

A *hero is someone we can admire without apology.*

—Kitty Kelley

Like Father—Like Son

His son, also named Joe, former All-Star guard of the Detroit Pistons, embodied that rare standard of talent, sportsmanship, and humility. He personifies the kind of adult that emerges when a father takes the job of raising his children seriously. His father is proof positive that a father's influence is born of *willingness,* not experience. He taught from the simple lesson book of action over words, substance over rhetoric. His legacy is preserved in the character and values of his children, whose lives were his sole priority.

There was little in young Joe Dumars Jr.'s life to indicate the kind of man he would become. He was abandoned by *his* father, raised by relatives and grew up amidst more neglect than love. Few would have been surprised if he had turned out hard and bitter. Too many American children seem unable to free themselves from the chains of their parents or the prisons of their childhood. To that end, Joe Jr. seemed an unlikely candidate to excel at family and fatherhood. But excel he did!

A *faith to live by, a self to live with, and a purpose to live for.*

—Bob Harrington

The Story of Cubby
"Hi Joe, Watcha Doin?"

Joe Dumars Jr. worked 60 to 80 hours a week as a truck driver to support his large family. Spare time was scarce and valuable as he truly cherished being with his wife and children. This scarcity of time made his influence on so many other young lives all the more amazing. It should also serve as a shameful reminder to *any* father who tries to use a scarcity of time as an excuse for neglect. As Joe Dumars would say . . *"that dog won't hunt!"*

"Joe would never ignore a child in need of even a few minutes of his time...or more," recalled his wife, Ophelia. "There was just something in his heart, something deep down and personal, as if he felt it was his moral responsibility to make a difference...when and where he could."

She recalled the story of Cubby to illustrate Joe's commitment to that ideal.

Ophelia remembers, "Cubby wandered over one day—Joe was sitting on the front porch—and hollered, 'Hi, Joe, watcha doin?' Joe took one look at Cubby and replied, 'Cubby, why aren't you wearing your shoes— it's cold out here today.' To which Cubby replied, 'Joe, I ain't got no shoes.'

"Well, that hit Joe real hard—he got this real troubled look on his face, personally feeling the pain of Cubby's plight. He really cared for Cubby.

"I remember Joe getting up from his chair and coming inside," Ophelia continued. "He came up to me and he said, 'Ophelia, I want you to go to the store and buy that boy a shirt, pants, belt, socks, underwear, and shoes.' He walked back out on the porch and hollered, 'Cubby, get yourself in this house right now!' When I returned Joe was just finishing up with Cubby in the bathtub—scrubbed him down good, really cleaned him up! Joe took Cubby into the living room and had him put on all these new clothes and then combed his hair real nice and stood back to take a look. I mean to tell you, that boy looked as snappy and proud as a peacock—never happier, and Joe says to him, 'Boy, you go on home now and show your mama how good you look!'

"Joe looked to me and smiled as he walked back out to the porch and the comfort of his chair. His eyes glowed and I know his heart was warmed. Cubby's new-found pride and happiness was Joe's too."

This is how lives are changed...one child at a time.

Joe's life stands in stark contrast to fathers accepting of low achievement expectations from their children. He'd have none of it! Joe's example also casts doubt on the belief that a child's early failures explain away the inability to cope and prosper as an adult.

His life should embarrass any young adult who believes his lack of success is not of his own making. Joe's legacy reminds all of us that there is no greater calling, no higher purpose, nothing as important as being a good father, solely dedicated to raising great kids.

The true measure of a man is gauged by his influence on the lives of children. By that standard Joe Dumars Jr. distinguished himself as few men ever do and helped define what it really means to be a man. As the Wizard of Oz shared with the Tin Man when he gave him his heart... "Remember, it is not how much we love but rather are loved by others that truly matters." Such was the legacy of kindness Joe Dumars, Jr. left in the lives of many.

CHAPTER 6

A CHAMPION'S EDUCATION

What Spectacle can be more edifying or more seasonable, than that of Liberty and Learning, each leaning on the other for their mutual and surest support?

James Madison

Education—Tyranny's Greatest Foe?

Ignorance and illiteracy have tethered far more slaves than shackles or chains. The world's tyrannical dictators have always feared thoughtfulness and collective knowledge over guns and swords. Revolutions find their roots in the inquisitive prowess of learned masses. The diffusion of education has always supported and enhanced freedom's cause.

And yet ignorance has tarnished events within our nation's borders by providing the impetus for some of *America's* most abhorrent and treacherous misconduct. Does the honor derived from the Revolutionary War balance the shame of the Salem witch burnings? A million Americans were killed liberating the world from communism, fascism, and nazism while simultaneously denying basic constitutional rights to members of its own citizenry. America's historical valor—and shame—has equal footing in education...or the lack thereof.

Both viewpoints support the indisputable importance and impact of education.

Upon the education of the people of this country, the fate of this country depends.

—Benjamin Disraeli

How Bad Is It?

The Federal Government recently appointed a blue-ribbon commission to conduct an objective and impartial evaluation of America's public educational system. It was comprised of some of our nation's brightest and most experienced parents, educators, and administrative officials.

The consensus was that the overall conditions of our public schools were shameful! They went on to say that if the current conditions had somehow been brought about by the actions of a hostile country, *it would be tantamount to an act of war!* The collective apathy and tolerance for the status quo—especially those kids trapped in the worst inner-city hellholes—defies explanation.

The ideal aim of education is the creation of power—of self control.
—John Dewey

The Greatest Personal Power

Power in America, or anywhere, is elusive to the uneducated. Armed with the basic, essential skills of reading and writing, no child's dreams should surpass their grasp. Now that's power—legitimate power! The ability to articulate and communicate dwarfs all else.

*F*or good or ill, your conversation is your advertisement. Every time you open your mouth you let men look into your mind. Do they see it well-clothed, neat, and professional?
—Bruce Burton

America's Unabated Blight

Fate routinely imparts ample random maliciousness to prove its impartiality. In fate's eyes—we are all equals.

Self-inflicted damage, resulting from bad judgment and poor decisions, is reaching *epidemic* proportions. Being struck by lightning is not synonymous with the pursuit of welfare saddled with an eighth-grade education. Fate and choice are vastly different circumstances.

Blaming our schools is convenient, and frequently legitimate, but if parents are failing anywhere—it's *right here and right now!*

I believe that schools exist to assist parents in the education of their children—not vice versa! Schools have our kids for six to eight hours a day, five days a week. The rest of the time they're with us.

If deficiencies are present—parents are the absolute last line of defense. Would you neglect to inoculate your children against deadly diseases? Why not treat ignorance and illiteracy as you would polio or smallpox?

Ignorance is a <u>voluntary</u> misfortune.

—Nicholas Ling

My Parents Blazed My Trail

Memories of my hometown's public library are among my most prized. It smelled like books, enveloped in the quiet of a confessional. Such an eclectic mixture of silence and knowledge provided a magical world for a seven-year-old boy to pass the day.

My parents are both deceased but the memories of our library excursions are rarely far from my thoughts. I smile as I think back to the late evenings I'd sit, impatient and restless, observing my parents check out ten books *each* to take home and read. It took years for me to understand and appreciate the true value of those outings.

Don't ask me who's influenced me. A lion is made up of the lambs he's digested, and I've been reading all my life.

—Giorgos Seferis

Your Vocabulary Defines You

I grew up with a passion for reading and a love of writing that has sustained me throughout my life. I observed that what people read had a profound impact on how they thought and the way they viewed the world. Deficiencies in either could also impact the way they view and judge their children.

My father was a newspaper editor. Throughout his life his grasp and understanding of the English language astonished me. I can't recall a single time he failed to answer my questions about grammar correctly. Not one single time. His confident and easy manner further frustrated my youthful attempts to trap him into a mistake. That was impressive—that was power! I began to recognize and understand the power that exceptional literacy could provide me.

There comes a time in every rightly constructed boy's life when he has a raging desire to go somewhere and dig for hidden treasure.

—Mark Twain

Don't Forget to Have Fun

Beyond the practical uses for literary skills—reading can be great fun! I take immense pleasure in watching my kids caught up in things they love. You instill in them the desire to read and you've issued them passports to endless and exciting journeys.

As a bored eight year old waiting for school to start, I relented and broke open Robinson Crusoe. It was my first literary experience absent Archie and Jughead.

I remember that day well. It was cool and overcast with the smell of a thunderstorm in the air. At that moment, a lifetime of reading pleasure came alive for me. Suddenly accessible were journeys, dreams, and adventures unimaginable to an eight year old. Nintendo is chump change to the magical excitement of *Treasure Island*. No digital gimmickry can recreate an H. G. Wells adventure. Sorry, Oprah—Mark Twain and Hemingway leave you in the dust. There is simply no substitute for the magical bedtime journey to *Pooh Corner* with good old Dad.

My son recently got his feet wet with his first computer game. Four nights running, the little guy has been trying to maneuver Buzz Lightyear past the enemy Zurg to rescue Woody from the evil toystore owner. I admit, I had mixed emotions watching him frenetically abusing my mouse. I relented only when persuaded that such exercise improves their hand-eye coordination. It's fun for him and the visual stimulation is a new dimension to explore and experience.

A few nights later, he asked if we could go upstairs and sit in "the big rocker" and read *Winnie the Pooh*. Up we went and twenty minutes later he was asleep in my arms, the two of us rocking gently with the still-open book in my lap. All I could hear was my son's soft breathing as I cradled his warm body in my arms and smelled his freshly bathed hair. His head was against my chest so I'm sure that whatever dreams he was having had his daddy's heartbeat for background music. At that moment it was clear to me that there is no substitute for *"the real thing...."*

As long as a man stands in his own way, everything seems to be in his way.

—Ralph Waldo Emerson

Disadvantaged or Disabled?

Don't you agree that it is sad and unfortunate that so many children are denied, or deny themselves, the happiness and pleasures associated with literacy? The tragedy, I believe, lies in the difficulty they will have finding personal and professional success without these skills and tools. The ability to articulate thoughts and clearly express ideas is so uncommon today that companies assign premiums to job candidates possessing them.

I once worked for a highly respected management-consulting firm staffed with the cream of the crop of professional and intellectual resources and talent. I recently had lunch with one of the senior partners who shared with me his frustration.

Attempting to promote national visibility among the firm's top performers the firm embarked upon a program where, weekly or monthly, these senior professionals researched and wrote essays, articles, or editorials, on particular subjects or issues. *"Steve, you can't believe the garbage that virtually every one of these otherwise stellar performers submitted for publication!"* Had they actually been submitted for publication the result would not have been national visibility but a one-way ticket back to junior high school for remedial education in reading and writing.

If our failing schools continue to produce more and more illiterate kids—reading and writing proficiency will *further* distinguish the "winners" from the "losers." It will also separate **the champions** from the also-rans.

To have another language is to possess a second soul.

—Charlemagne

Are We Dooming New Arrivals?

People from all over the world are increasingly flocking to America to seize upon her vast economic opportunities. Immigrants all— motivated by a single hope, a common purpose the pursuit of the American dream of freedom, riches, and success.

Upon arrival, most people quickly discover that here they are, in America, *and they can't speak English.* It's clear that our misguided efforts to accommodate multiple language needs actually *hinder* their prospects for success. Don't get me wrong.

I'm not suggesting that we deny these foreign kids and their parents the means and resources necessary to learn English. I'm referring to advocates of "bilingual" education, where the primary obstacle, fluency in English, is unnecessarily delayed. The only prayer for success these folks will ever have is the rapid assimilation of the English language.

Like it or not, this country functions and operates in English. Immigrant parents, who want access to America's opportunities, need to make two commitments. Number one is to get their kids in an English language immersion program as quickly as possible. Secondly, make the commitment to learn our language themselves. The best jobs go to the students who have acquired English language skills and are well spoken and articulate.

You want the key to all America's vaults? Would you like to share in the riches, the opportunities, and the lifestyle? *Commit and dedicate yourselves to learning how to read and write in English as quickly as you can.* Good things will follow.

The ignorant continue to be in the hands of the foolish. Advocates of "cultural diversity" over accelerated English literacy are sentencing immigrants to chronic unemployment or under-employment, low self-esteem, and self-imposed restrictions from the best things America has to offer them. How good will they feel about themselves then? It's worth repeating—*learning the English language is your best shot at the brass ring.*

*Hear me now! Without a good education...
You're not going anywhere in this world!*

—Malcolm X

A Tragedy of National Scope . . .

An American tragedy continues to unfold before our eyes. Increasingly, we are denying our respective American birthright by promoting cultural differences over our historical citizenry.

For example, it is indisputable that the freedom, progress, and opportunities gained by African Americans in the last hundred years were commensurate with their increased rates of literacy. Literacy was, *and still is,* the single most powerful weapon they had in accessing the American dream. During the years of slavery, African Americans were denied, *by law,* the right of education and thus the power of literacy. The slave owners understood. (They were *educated.*) They knew that with education came power and with it the shackles of slavery could not hold back the dreams of African American families!

It's troubling to me why more minority families with school-age children, trapped in inner-city "school-prisons" don't demand alternative choices. I read recently that children in these inner-city schools have a greater chance of becoming victims of a violent crime than they do of graduating from high school. That is a shameful, national disgrace—pure and simple!

Education is the ability to meet life's situations.

—Dr. John G. Hibben

Dads—Just Do It!

Read to them every day when they're young. Take them to libraries and turn them loose in this magical new world. Encourage them to write about anything they desire or can imagine. As their enthusiasm grows...fan those passions! Stoke their fires of curiosity and creativity. Arm them with the grammar and composition skills of an American champion. Quiz them, drill them, scrutinize them, challenge them, and push them as hard as you can to become exceptional writers and insatiable readers. Success will be hard to avoid when your children are equipped with the *right* tools.

The greatest reward your children will realize from your unwavering efforts will be that someday they will be able to take a bedtime journey to Pooh Corner with children of their own and, like the title of the movie, "That's as good as it gets!"

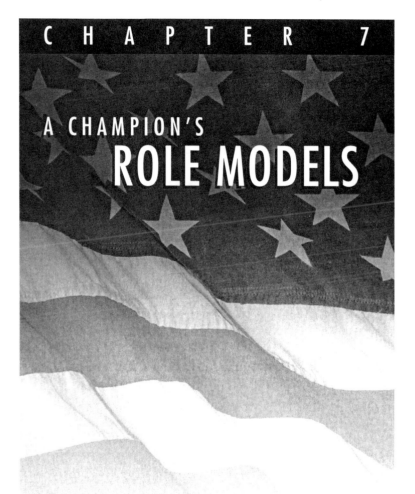

CHAPTER 7

A CHAMPION'S
ROLE MODELS

*When I was coaching, the one
thought that I would try to get across
to my players was that everything
I do each day, everything I say,
I must first think what effect it
will have on everyone concerned.*

Frank Layden

Where Have Our Heroes Gone?

Every generation has a surplus of "heroes" to idolize and emulate. Mine was no exception. Most adults of my generation had *some* redeeming value that they were willing to contribute. Even the *rough* characters sensed an obligation to at least *attempt* to steer us straight. They'd be drinking and smoking and swearing and then chastise *us* for lying, yelling at our parents, or missing school. There was a measure of empathy in *everyone*.

For whatever reason, it's *different* today. As in the past...we have famous people *ideally* suited to act as strong and positive role models...*but simply choose not to*. This void only *heightens* the necessity of fathers assuming this critical role. I'm troubled when I see athletic superstars like Basketball Hall-of-Famer Charles Barkley's infamous declaration, *"I ain't no role model!"* I can't envision Bart Starr or Roger Staubach abdicating in such a reckless and careless manner.

Children have more need of models than of critics.

—Carolyn Coats

YOU—Show Them How...

Children will always do as we do...not as we <u>say</u>. To a child, Dad embodies all that is right and good. Aside from Mom, he's the most influential figure in that child's life. This is a huge obligation—one that lasts a lifetime. It's not easy to live up to, but we must! Children see and copy every single thing we do.

LITTLE EYES UPON YOU

There are little eyes upon you
and they're watching night and day.
There are little ears that quickly
take in every word you say.
There are little hands all eager
to do anything you do;
And a little boy who's dreaming
of the day he'll be like you.

You're the little fellow's idol,
you're the wisest of the wise.
In his little mind about you
no suspicions ever rise.
He believes in you devoutly,
holds all that you say and do;
He will say and do, in your way,
when he's grown up just like you.

There's a wide-eyed little fellow
who believes you're always right;
And his eyes are always opened,
as he watches you day and night.
You are setting an example
every day in all you do,
For the little boy who's waiting

to grow up to be like you......

Well done is better than well said.

—Benjamin Franklin

They're Going to Be Just Like...You

How many kids who smoke had fathers that smoked? How many drunks raised alcoholic teenagers? How many bullies had abusive fathers? How many children, with dads parked in front of the TV, ever visit libraries? How many children are born bigots? How much hatred is learned... *from observing?*

They look up to you. They idolize you. They want to be like you. They mimic and copy every single thing that you do. They are your legacy—your ultimate societal contribution. Make it count!

Take good hold of instruction and don't let her go, keep her for she is your life.

—The Bible

Communicate—Tell Them Why

Too many parents confuse *babbling* with talking and gibberish with communication. It's crucial that we talk *and* communicate...now more than ever. I always take the time to sit my kids down, have them look me in the eyes, and explain important things to them in a simple and direct manner. *"Do you understand?"* They'll nod and you're never quite sure if they got it but they're developing critical skills... listening, learning, and communicating.

*F*aith is power to believe and
power to see...

— Prentice Mulford

When television arrived a small boy was asked, "So, son, now that you've experienced television, which do you like better, the television or the radio?"

The boy lit up and unhesitatingly offered up his answer, "Oh, radio, mister, it's a lot better—it has much better pictures!"

In a digital culture becoming visually supersonic, we mustn't abandon our own imagination as our dream's guiding light.

The lines between fantasy and reality are narrowing. I'm very consistent in pointing out and explaining why certain behaviors are good and bad. "Braden, see how that boy opened that door for that older man who isn't feeling well? That's a nice thing to do and that boy is probably a very nice boy."

He nodded and later in the day he held open a door at the gym for everyone who walked through for the next ten minutes. The smiles, the thanks, and the pats on the head were all the reward he needed. He was beginning to understand...

Communication is depositing a part of yourself in another person.

—Source Unknown

Communicate—Tell Them Why

Today's lack of role models is a legitimate debate. What's indisputable is the abundance of negative, destructive, and immoral temptations permeating the lives of our kids, vying for _both_ their attention and money.

I don't blame Hollywood or Nintendo for negatively influencing my kids, and any father complaining about what his kids play or watch should spend more time at home disposing of it. As a father...I would be embarrassed beyond words to infer that my kids were more influenced by junk than by me. That responsibility lies squarely on my shoulders and the shoulders of all responsible fathers. If it doesn't pass my standards it's gone or turned off. Pretty simple. If exposure to this offensive stuff is so detrimental, why aren't more parents controlling access and exposure to it?

If you sleep in trash cans —don't be surprised if you wake up smelling like garbage. As my children's father, until I believe they possess the maturity and judgment to evaluate the worth of some of this weird stuff, I *will* control their access and exposure to it.

So, Mom and Dad—instead of complaining about what they're watching, just turn it off!

How's YOUR Photo Album? (Click)

The world was forever changed when George Eastman introduced us to cameras and film. Imagine! Aim a box with a lens and capture a moment in time forever. Freeze fragments of family history for future generations to view and enjoy. The album's integrity would be dependent upon the character behind the camera.

Was Eastman so clever? Since the dawn of time children have similarly recorded "fragments" of their lives, etched in their own vivid memories, compiling their own family albums.

Don't Just Say It…DO IT! (Click)

What indelible images mark the albums of <u>your</u> kids? *Click* How many children have witnessed Dad hitting Mom? Is there a photo of Dad passed out on the couch or not leaving a tip for the waitress? *Click* How many fathers utter racial slurs in front of their kids in anger or frustration? *Click* How often does a son or daughter witness Dad calling in sick from work only to go fishing or drinking? *Click* Is this the kind of "photo album" you want your child referencing into adulthood? Are these the moments you want them remembering and imitating?

How about a *better* photo album? **Click** There's one of Dad hugging and kissing Mom. **Click** Look there's a nice one of Dad stopping to help someone in distress. **Click** "Hey, Dad just gave back ten dollars to the clerk who miscounted his change!" **Click** "Dad came home early today to help Mom and then he's taking us all to dinner and a ball game!

Every minute with your kids is a potential Kodak moment. You need to be aware and on your best behavior because you never know when they'll be **Click** taking pictures that will frame their adult judgment and context about things. Be careful what gets recorded in *your* family's film.

It is easier to exemplify values than teach them.

—Theodore M. Hesburgh

Touchdown!

Many of today's role models have abandoned the opportunity to be a positive example to kids desperately needing one. Sure, always there are notable exceptions—athletes who understand that "little eyes upon them" embodies an obligation to conduct themselves with dignity and responsibility. I don't know if it's the money, the notoriety, or what today. Relatively speaking, yesterday's stars acted and behaved with an agreeable level of class and decorum—understanding the great influence they had on America's youth.

THE BRIDGE BUILDER

An old man going down a lone highway
Came in the evening cold and gray
To a chasm vast and deep and wide
Through which was flowing a sullen tide.
The old man crossed in the twilight dim;
That swollen stream held no fears for him;
But he turned when safe on the other side
And built a bridge to span the tide.

"Old man, said a fellow pilgrim near,
"You are wasting your strength with building here;
Your journey will end with the ending day;
You never again must pass this way;
You have crossed the chasm deep and wide—
Why build you this bridge at eventide?"

The builder lifted his old gray head.
"Good friend, in the path I have come," he said,
"There followeth after me today,
A youth whose feet must pass this way.
This swollen stream which was naught to me
To that fair-haired youth may a pitfall be;
He too must cross in the twilight dim;
Good friend, I'm building this bridge for him."

We should all always remember to go forward with an eye behind us to those just beginning or discovering their *own* journeys.

CHAPTER 8

A CHAMPION'S
RESPECT

*Men are respectable only if
they respect.*

Ralph Waldo Emerson

Where We Are Today

Few traditional American values have been immune to the cultural erosion we're experiencing. Respect, or the lack thereof, tops the list. Look around you. The last fifty years have seen a wholesale abandonment of exhibiting proper homage and respect to the things that used to mean something. Like most plagues, this malaise is rarely recognized in time to control or manage its destructive tendencies. Merely surviving it, ultimately, becomes the primary objective. Indifference to this cultural virus could be our nation's undoing.

The flip side of respect is disrespect and is clearly the root cause of our worst problems. Consider:

■ Teachers once represented the cream of our intellectual and ethical base. The erosion of respect diminished their influence and control in the classroom effectively removing their sole reason for becoming teachers. The current state of public education is evidence of the impact.

■ Television continues its slide into the sewer as networks compete on shock value and slime content rather than substance to demonstrate their respect for us.

■ CEOs of major American companies have shown their respect for stockholders by looting these firms of billions of dollars while Joe Average watches his 401(k) become worthless.

■ Elected officials show their respect for us through deceit and dishonesty.

■ Public discourse is increasingly laced with profanities and racial epithets.

Around the world the American military is vilified, threatened, and criticized, by the very nations that have, and will again, beg us to intervene on their behalf when rhetoric becomes useless in the face of evil power.

When was the last time a kid held a door open for you?

We as a people have become rude, obnoxious, and disrespectful. The admired and widely exhibited traits of our ancestors—dignity, class, courtesy, graciousness, and respect—are being nudged aside by rudeness, apathy, insolence, and *disrespect*. It's more than a societal blemish—it's a cultural fungus.

My good manners aren't genetic. I was fortunate to have a father who was, like most of the men of his generation, a gentleman. He was a gentleman with respect, concern, and regard for other people. The irony is that the act of extending respect makes me feel good! I pity children denied this legal intoxication because of fathers who didn't teach them how to do it.

Respect. Teach them that only its extension assures its return. "Yes sir," "No sir," "Thank you, you're welcome," are not just good manners but a visible X-ray of our character.

The way to procure insults is to submit them; a man meets with no more respect than he exacts.

—William Hazlitt

Is There an Explanation?

What's happening to us? Why the collapse of our collective standards? The answers are pretty clear and evident if we just examine the things we accept today as *normal*.

Today's role models or maybe the shortage of them are partially to blame. America's heroes have always pulled double-duty in acting as role models to the day's youth. It's only natural that kids want to be *like Mike*. All of us remember someone who mastered his craft and the public with equal aplomb.

Do we have fewer legitimate role models today? Are current role models the cause or are they symptomatic of something else?

The Failure Is the Father's

Sorry, Dad, the buck stops here. In every family I spoke with for this book I asked who their heroes were. There was no debate—just consensus. They all assigned hero status to their father, someone they looked up to, admired, and emulated. This is the kind of power and influence needed to shape lives and provide the moral leadership and guidance to this generation.

Avoid being the father assured a torturous future because of an irresponsible past. Do it right the first time and enjoy the future together.

Sports Heroes

Taunting and ridiculing opponents is becoming commonplace in the sports world. I don't think I need to elaborate on the spectacle of a seven-year-old Pee Wee Leaguer pounding his chest and sticking his finger in the face of his opponent. If you can't appreciate and understand the nature and ramifications of this disrespectful gesture...you just don't get it.

Bob Costas, America's premier sportscaster, said it best during a recent interview when he stated profoundly and incredulously, "Don't these guys watch classic sports films of past sports heroes? Can't they see that Gale Sayers or Jim Brown calmly and casually handing the football to the referee after scoring is way, *way* cooler than *any* of the loud, showboating antics of today's players?"

Shut up and hand the ball to the ref! You'll do more to restore respect in our young people than all their teachers combined.

Entertainment

What kid isn't sick of hearing his parents wistfully reminiscing about how great things were "in the good old days"? Yeah, right. I'm sure our children are heartbroken about the lack of black and white television, calculators, computers, and digital technology.

Hollywood has never been noted for its temperance and ignores any notion of social responsibility. Little of what oozes out of it today is thoughtful or of any social value. How far have we sunk? In 1964, the Beatles took America by storm with such lyrics, as "I want to hold your hand," and were considered *extreme* and *sinful* by parents of that era.

A mere forty years later popular bands promulgate lyrics that celebrate violence, abuse of women, murdering cops, and rape, and contain more profanity than an Oakland Raiders home game, and they claim they're mainstream.

I would like to share an important idea with all parents. Forget the V-Chip and just turn it off!

Businesses and Business Leaders . . .

In the 1960s it was aerospace. In the seventies it was oil. In the go-go eighties it was mergers and acquisitions. In the nineties it was high-tech and dot.com mania. Today it's anything goes.

We're not entitled to piously lecture our young on the virtues of honesty and integrity if we don't practice it in our business affairs. As responsible fathers we need to set an example by patronizing the businesses that promote and reflect our own values in their workplace.

Politicians . . .

Political discourse and debate anchors our democratic system of government. Local and national politics is the means by which we shape our collective ambitions and implement action that preserves our future.

As Americans, we need to take the initiative and demand civil, honest, and *respectful* discourse in the national debate. Contrary to the beliefs of some... character does matter.

. . . and Finally Teachers

Teachers, in terms of influencing respect, are as much a part of the problem as they are a part of the solution. What do I mean by that?

The quality of teaching and the quality of teachers is dropping like a rock. The good ones are retiring in record numbers and the "best and brightest" of the future are opting for stock options in Silicon Valley, leaving us with too large a percentage of teachers who pursued teaching by default or as a last resort. The lack of respect—sometimes even the promotion of it—is occurring on their watch.

Thankfully, there are still many exceptional and dedicated teachers striving daily to survive an impossible situation. Monopolistic governmental bureaucracies, rather than the teachers and parents, are developing and administering scholastic curriculums. I sincerely sympathize with teachers. It wasn't that many years ago that a career in teaching was enthusiastically pursued by America's best and brightest who now shun it.

We need to restore teaching to a career of the highest order and honor, which is respected by students and parents alike. It's not too late but it's getting closer to midnight.

Respect commands itself and can neither be Given nor withheld when it is due.
—Eldridge Cleaver

Respect Comes in Many Shapes and Sizes

Respect covers a broad spectrum of behavior and circumstances. There are things in our lives that we naturally hold in high regard, in high esteem...with *respect,* because it's the right thing to do. Flags should not be burned. Adults should get deference. Legal authority should be observed and obeyed. That's why it's so important to frame all of their messages in the context of respect.

Self-Respect

It all starts here. Self-respect is the epicenter of their being. Its presence or absence will determine their future. People lacking it have trouble extending it. That reduces the odds of them receiving it and thus the cycle continues.

On this issue, I find myself in rare agreement with many social psychologists. Children raised in a non-nurturing environment become adults with little empathy and compassion. They also become more vulnerable to membership in the school of "victimology." Once enrolled there, you'll never be at fault for anything as long as you live.

All kids have emotional piggy banks. Investing in it regularly ensures security when withdrawals are demanded. Get them two piggy banks in case one is not enough.

Respect For Adults

Respecting adults ranked high for the families in this book. These fathers brooked no nonsense here. Unequivocally, they believed that respect for adults was a bedrock principle that couldn't be compromised. Their sons and daughters agreed, maintaining that any act of disrespect to any adult meant swift and harsh punishment—and I agree.

We accept that violent criminals who attempt to kill police officers are decidedly more dangerous than other criminals. Clearly, someone dangerous and deranged enough to shoot a cop has few limits to his potential for violence.

Applying the same standard, doesn't a youngster with no respect for adults represent a bigger threat to others their own age? If only to minimize threats to their peers, swift and decisive punishment for any disrespect to adults is a critical responsibility.

A faithful friend is a strong defense: and he that hath found one hath found a treasure.

—The Bible

Respect for Friends

We take many things for granted. Friendship should not be one of them. True and devoted friendships are rare and should be cherished and protected as we would a fine jewel. Teach your children that acquaintances are plentiful—especially when we're young, but true friends are rare and should never be taken for granted, only respected.

Respect America...Your Country

With all her warts, America is still the best place on earth to live and work. Apathy and lack of proper respect for our country among children is proof of a deficient education in their own history. If our kids better understood and respected their own birthright they'd surely have more respect for one another. Dads? That's your job too. Don't hesitate to wrap them up in the American flag!

A gentleman is someone who considers the rights of others before his own feelings, and the feelings of others before his own rights.

—John Wooden

Respect All People

Persuade children to extend respect to everyone. Our country's become culturally diversified to the point of near ruin. Let me explain.

We all have different backgrounds and ethnic roots and we should certainly encourage our kids to explore and learn about them. Genealogy isn't just fascinating, it can be tremendously liberating and interesting— *in its proper context.*

But when these cultural identities and distinctions take priority over the distinction and meaning of being an American citizen, nothing good will come from it. This nation expanded and achieved greatness by respecting and honoring individual rights, the rights of Americans—not by foolishly and endlessly accommodating every dissenting group of malcontents.

Respect. Who we are is best measured in terms of the respect we extend and receive. It's an accurate measure of our humanity and national character. Your kids are the first, of many, bricks.

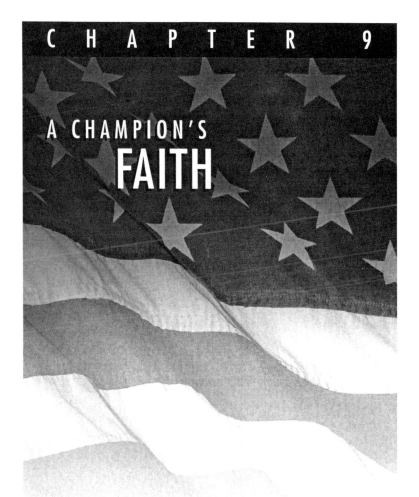

CHAPTER 9

A CHAMPION'S
FAITH

*Faith is deliberate confidence in the
character of God whose ways you
may not understand at the time.*

Oswald Chambers

One Nation—Under God

Due to its vital importance, I labored over how to present this chapter without risking the integrity and credibility of the book's central theme—fathers raising champion citizens. Religious debate seems to trigger so much rancor and emotion.

Religion is also such an intensely personal subject that discussing it always runs the risk of being misinterpreted or highly scrutinized.

In the end, I felt that a discussion on the value, merits, and role of religion in bringing up our children would not risk the integrity of my message—it would *ensure* it.

Man does what he can...
God does what he will.

—Proverb

Where Are We Today...and Why?

The declining values of America's youth coincide with the diminishing presence and role of the church in our traditional institutions. A partial explanation is the concerted efforts of anti-religious groups to de-legitimize religion on multiple fronts.

The groups base their criticisms on the inaccurate belief that America's Constitution demands the separation of church and state. Aided by the American Civil Liberties Union and activist judges, their efforts are causing irreparable harm to the moral infra-structure of our country. Simultaneously, they *promote* many of the activities and beliefs *contrary* to the moral values of the majority of the people. Is it any wonder our kids are marginalizing things like the Ten Commandments when public access to them has been systematically stifled?

> **G**od brings men into deep waters
> not to drown them but to cleanse them.
>
> —John Hugh Aughey

But, What Does Religion Change?

Why is the public presence of religion so important to raising good kids into exceptional adults? The answer is *influence,* a strong, positive, and virtuous *influence* in a culture rife with *negative* influences.

Every family I interviewed for this book believed that their religious associations were major influences on their children's moral foundation and developing character. *Every single one of them!*

I consider myself a non-denominational Christian though I was raised in a Roman Catholic family. The church influenced my belief that a far greater authority than man would someday judge the way I'd lived my life. It didn't *always* keep me out of trouble but it established reasonable standards of behavior when it mattered most. Kids of any era will push the envelope of danger and delinquency. Religion tempers youthful indiscretions and exuberance through its moral and authoritative *influence*.

The frightening difference between today's kids and those of just a generation or two ago strongly supports my contention. The collective lack of respect for human life by young adults has skyrocketed. Most inner cities have become drug-plagued battle zones. Children have been conditioned to casually accept the likelihood that they will be murdered before their twenty-first birthday. But this problem is not isolated. It is also becoming increasingly common in middle-class suburbs. Nice neighborhoods where, until recently, such incidents were rare. It doesn't take a genius to recognize a mounting vacuum of moral turpitude.

Like a city whose walls are broken down is a man who lacks self control.

— Proverbs 25:28

What's Doing This to Our Kids?

Opinions vary as to what's causing this massive erosion in our moral values. "Expert" opinions (guesses) run the gamut. They include the desensitization to death from years of watching violence on TV and at the movies. High on the list are homes absent full-time fathers. Drugs? Peer pressure?

Or maybe just a lack of respect for the things in life that used to matter.

Clearly, some or all of these examples are contributing factors. I find it curious and troubling that the growing absence of religion isn't discussed more as a legitimate cause. At-risk kids care little about God's wrath if they're unaware of his existence.

To me, it is incomprehensible that this level of crime and violence could exist among young people versed in the teachings of Jesus Christ.

Scarier yet is the seemingly casual acceptance of religion's federally-mandated exclusion from places it's needed most. This PC-driven mandate may be costing us more young lives than guns and drugs combined! What reasonable parent actually believes that children glancing at a plaque of the Ten Commandments in a public school are being harmed, or offended, or that it represents a threat to our Constitution? It defies rational explanation.

Nothing hath separated us from God but our own will, or rather our own will is our separation from God.

—William Law

PSSST! It's Not True!

Separation of church and state has become a rallying cry for a legion of disparate public interests. It is currently defined as "governmentally-mandated absence of any religious overtones, anywhere, anytime—where public facilities are part of the mix."

What this phrase really means is *the separation of our country from its heritage*. The notion that the first amendment disallows the *presence* of religion in the public domain, i.e., schools, government, armed forces, courts, etc., is simply incorrect. Over the last half-century federal courts have incrementally relented to anti-religious groups in *reinterpreting* the Constitution. In so doing they have effectively altered America's cultural and social landscape. The casualties have been America's families. Hardest hit have been America's children.

To better understand the implications and impact of this kind of judicial intervention and subsequent "invention" of *new* Constitutional rights, consider that the *right* to an abortion and the *right* to affirmative action and the *right* to be forcibly bused to schools and the *right* not to be exposed to religion in the public domain, all had one very important and disturbing common denominator: None originated in any legislature nor were voted on by citizenry most subject to its impact. Every one of these new Constitutional *rights* was created by judicial fiat by judges seeking to bend the Constitution to their own philosophical ends. Constitutional law wasn't a factor in their decisions. Constitutional rights can be counterfeited, and widely distributed, before the rest of us ever see it coming.

The United States was built on a fundamental belief in the word of God. Virtually every significant historical document makes reference to our faith in, respect for, and reverence to the Creator. Our founding fathers looked to God for strength and inspiration. Our currency bears the inscription *In God we trust* and our courts require that witnesses, with hand on the Holy Bible, swear to tell the truth, *"...so help me God."* And finally, the "Pledge of Allegiance" to these United States, recited by our children—hands over their hearts—concludes with the phrase, *One nation— under God, indivisible, with liberty and justice for all.*

Men must be governed by God, or they will be ruled by tyrants.

—William Penn

So, What Happened?

A scant forty-two years ago, President Dwight Eisenhower proudly proclaimed after signing into law that national reference to the Almighty in the "Pledge of Allegiance"—*From this day forward, the millions of our young school children will daily proclaim in every city and town, in every village and rural school house, the dedication of our nation and our people to the Almighty.*

How is it possible that in the few short years that have passed since Ike echoed that historic pro-clamation we have all but purged *any* reference to God from the vocabulary of our public institutions— especially in our schools, where we need it most? It's not just curious or politically correct—it is in fact...*harmful and disgraceful!*

The Christian is not one who has gone all the way with Christ. None of us has. The Christian is one who has found the right road.

—Charles L. Allen

Isn't This All Getting a Little Silly?

During the last fifty years, courts and judges have attempted to reshape our society's values through *"tortured interpretations"* of long-standing Constitutional law. These black-robed wise men and women have taken us from a time when prayer was encouraged and practiced in the classroom to today, where some blind guy negotiating the hallways to traffic court hits the ACLU lottery jackpot. In his lawsuit he's seeking significant punitive damages resulting from an incident where he overheard "Silent Night" being played softly in the courthouse bathroom.

So now separation of church and state, as applied to education, means that a moment of thanks or prayer at a graduation ceremony is uncon-stitutional. It also means that students may not pause for a moment of silence at the beginning of their school day. It means that a nativity scene may not be displayed on public property unless there are other displays (e.g., Santa Claus or Christmas trees) that secularize the presentation, due to the possibility that someone, somewhere, somehow, may be *offended* at the sight of a baby surrounded by barn animals and three old guys.

God hears no more than the heart speaks; And if the heart be dumb, God will certainly be deaf.

—Thomas Brooks

An Important Distinction . . .

I would respectfully encourage all of you to understand that the separation of church and state is not actually a law. It is a doctrine, a legal concept that has been implemented by the various courts, primarily over the last fifty years. If this concept, as originally understood, had been applied with consistency over the years, America would certainly be a different country right now. Religious expression would flourish, and the courts would not be micro-managing the religious life of the American people, and increasingly putting our children into harm's way.

The doctrine of separation of church and state is being used to effectively purge religion from the public square. The historical perspective on church/state issues reveals a much different story. The government was to *accommodate* the religious communities; religion and religious expression were to be encouraged. For example, this is why the first Congress asked President George Washington to issue a Thanksgiving Proclamation upon completion of the Bill of Rights. In our current climate of political correctness that practice would be viewed as unconstitutional. It would violate currently held views (still inaccurate) on the separation of church and state.

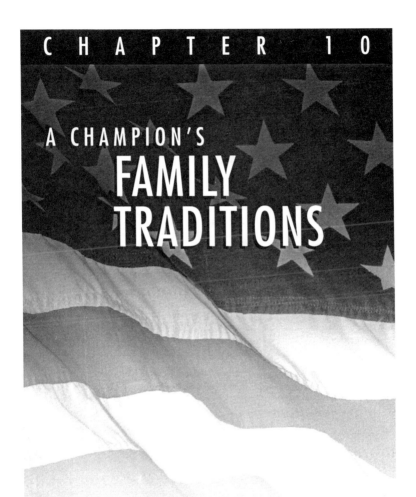

CHAPTER 10

A CHAMPION'S
FAMILY
TRADITIONS

What an enormous magnifier is tradition! How a thing grows in the human memory and in the human imagination, when love, worship, and all that lies in the human heart, is there to encourage it.

Thomas Carlyle

Good morning, yesterday
You wake up and time
has slipped away.
And suddenly it's hard to find
The memories you left behind
Remember, do you remember. . .
the times of your life?"

You might remember these lyrics from Paul Anka's timeless classic. It was also Kodak's brilliant theme song for a decade. It perfectly captures and defines life's best moments. It also assigns great value to these memories as our lives near closure.

As the years pass by, I'm increasingly comforted by thoughts of the past—special memories of family occasions and celebrated events. What made them special was more the anticipation leading up to them than the actual events. Be it Thanksgiving dinner at Grandma's house or the regular Wednesday night outings to McDonalds or Pizza Hut, it was special in large part because we could *depend* on it. It was something we looked forward to and cherished—moments we'll always remember.

Family traditions are more than the sporadic or random consumption of time doing *whatever.* Traditional activities provide us the opportunity to unite together for a common purpose, build solid emotional bonds that will last a lifetime, and create an atmosphere of *stability.* That stability provides our children the secure foundation upon which their lives will be built.

*Recollection is the only paradise from
Which we cannot be turned out.*

      — Jean Paul Richter

So, What's the Big Deal?

It's important that children have things they can count on. Things like traditional family events. A child's stability stems in large part from trust. When children know that certain family celebrations and events are guaranteed they gain confidence. They also develop a sense of trust in parents who deliver and keep their word. Assign the same value to these special occasions as you would in building a strong mooring for a ship in rough seas and you'll begin to appreciate their critical value. They need things to rely on in an unreliable world.

These special moments will also feed their souls someday in times of crisis or tragedy. Paul Anka was right when he sang, "...memories are times that you borrow...to spend when you get to tomorrow." Someday we'll all need as much of this currency as we can lay our hands on. Make sure you don't leave your children short. Give them a memory chest that's stuffed to the hilt.

*Tradition does not mean that the living
are dead, but that the dead are living.*

—Gilbert K. Chesterton

Where Do I Start?

Family traditions run the gamut. You could have three old men reminiscing on the porch about their most cherished family memories. The guy from Alaska tears up, remembering that last walrus he and Gramps slaughtered. They were flush with whale fat for a year! "Pops" Welch, formerly of New Orleans, gets a lump in his throat remembering those trips to the jazz bars with Dad—when he was 8. "Old Bones" Snyder, formerly of San Francisco, quick-draws his hanky and blows, overcome with flashbacks of those cool, foggy evenings with Dad, launching rotten tomatoes during the GOP primaries.

Family traditions start with individual family choices based on countless factors unique to each of us. Most traditions will likely share some of the following characteristics:

- The events are enjoyable and memorable.
- They normally seek to promote core family values and beliefs.
- They are preceded by some shared anticipation.
- They are regular and consistent.
- They promote family love and bonds.
- They create strong and vivid memories that will last a lifetime.
- They teach valuable "life lessons" while providing varied experiences.
- They encourage everyone's enthusiastic input.

These family traditions are entirely about spending regular quality time with our children. A life that ends deplete of special memories is a sad and wasted existence. Immunize yourself and your children against such an outcome.

Other things may change us,
But we start and end as family.

—Anthony Brandt

Some Ideas . . .

Here are a few of my own ideas for traditional events. They're a mixed bag from a number of sources including my own young life. One is no better than another. My only wish is that reading them might motivate fathers to action for their own young children.

Holidays

Holidays, such as Christmas, Thanksgiving, Fourth of July, Easter, etc., are a chance to teach your children the history and meaning of each holiday. When they see you practicing kindness and generosity you won't need to promote it—they'll understand.

Birthdays

Don't childhood birthdays rule? They rank up there with our best-ever moments! What a concept! A national day of recognition for *me!* People bringing *me* gifts from *my* wish list and hanging around long enough to see *me* play with them. A table full of foods normally denied me to stuff myself with. For that one day a year I make the sun stand in line because everything else is orbiting around me.

Well, at least that's the way I remember it. The key is to make whoever's birthday it is **feel** like they're **IT**, the most important person on the block, for at least 24 hours.

Family Trips

Parents everywhere should strongly resist all lengthy family trips in their automobiles. While I recognize that the annual cross-country marathon is an American rite of passage, resist the temptation.

Why am I so negative about these trips? My dourness was shaped in August of 1964 when I was nine. For reasons still unknown, my dad decided it was time for me to see Disneyland. Sounded great. Wait a minute...how many miles between Denver and Los Angeles?

He also decided he could kill two birds with one stone by detouring through Tucson to visit our Aunt Edna...in mid-August. And finally, the vehicle whisking us to Magic Mountain was a 1964 Oldsmobile Jet Star-88—with no air conditioner.

The final outcome was the worst tradeoff since the Indians sold New York for twelve bucks and some beads. My four-hour "dream" time at Disneyland was balanced out nicely by nine days in the 114-degree back seat of the heat-absorbing Oldsmobile. A dwindling supply of glazed donuts and a half pint of warm milk were my sole companions.

Einstein was right. Time bends to eternity as evidenced by my family hurtling through Mojave Desert at just under the legal speed limit.

And don't even get me started on those KOA campgrounds.

Anyway, that's how I remember it. I'm sure it was worse but I've blocked out the bad parts. The choice regarding this American ritual is all yours. My kids will be airplane-bound, rent-a-car chauffeured, and Marriott-housed at our points of destination. Child abuse laws are much stricter today so I'm not taking any chances.

Relatives

On any scale the twentieth century was an historical miracle. Among its relatively few minuses was the resultant loss of contact with close family members. Small agricultural communities gave way to a modern societal and industrial transformation that separated families on a grand scale. America lost something in the process.

My mother was eccentric but, in her own abstract way, wise. She felt that our quality of life could be compared to a mighty river. Just as a river is nourished and strengthened by the many small tributaries that flow into it, so also are our lives. To my mother, life's tributaries consisted of our family tree and circle of friends and events.

Could our cultural decline be traced to the number of these "tributaries" that have been cut off? When a river dries up, drought and destruction follow. Could our troubled youth be dying of thirst?

Fathers need to monitor the river's flow. Put in human terms, you wouldn't drink from a river that is downstream to a chemical factory. Why allow garbage movies, low-character friends, or any other negative pollution through your doors.

At Home

Disneyland or McDonald's aside, spending time with your son or daughter clutching your chest in the rocking chair, stroking their heads, reveling in the scent of their hair, sharing soft words or songs, and knowing that these moments are beautiful but fleeting, represent the very best in the creation of pleasant family memories. While Disneyland or Christmas may look and feel like a ten-dollar bill— the accrual of these smaller "pennies" allows us to become rich over a lifetime.

Make things fun and enjoyable for them. Their appreciation of the trivial isn't trivial.

Recreational

I grew up as a hard-core athlete. I still believe that life's important lessons can be gleaned from a ball field. Sports are a great teacher of teamwork, dealing with loss, respect for authority, the value of practice and commitment, and the promotion of sportsmanship. But that's not my main point.

Aside from the value of competition and recreation, basic fitness is life enhancing. The de-emphasis of athletics by adults is partially to blame for today's fatter kids. Athletics was always important but participation in fitness activities was more widely promoted and practiced.

Create activities that allow your child to experience exercise and fitness without the pressure of competition. That will come along all too soon.

- Take them on little hiking excursions.
- Go swimming.
- Teach them to ride bikes and then go with them.
- Kids love to climb—promote it and explore various avenues of doing it.
- I always let my kids "help" me by carrying stuff into or around the house. I don't really need the help but they love giving it—and they enjoy the excursions.

You get the point. Get off the couch and go outside with them.

Excursions

I once had a Golden retriever named Winston. His most endearing trait was his frenzied joy and excitement at the prospect of going *anywhere* in the car! He didn't care where, when, how long...he just wanted to go with me.

Garry Shandling had a great story on just this topic. "My dog Shepp loved to get into and out of the car. I hated to drive so I would park the car in the driveway, open both back doors and whistle for Shepp. He would run out all excited, climb up into the car—sit down, and then get out of the car on the other side! I would go in the house and Shepp would do this all day long."

My kids are same way. Kids don't care where you're going, they're just certain of two things: they're with you and they'll probably see or experience something new. Never give them a reason not to want to make the trip with you.

Every Saturday morning my dad would take me with him to Montgomery Wards for a two hour "look around." He never bought anything, just looked around. I don't think he took me along for companionship...I think Mom made him. Which was fine with me. The giant bag of malt balls I demanded to accompany him was more than a fair trade. He got to look around for two hours while I watched cartoons on 500 TVs while devouring a pound of candy. When Dad was ready to leave, he had the store public-address announcer broadcast his location so I wouldn't miss my ride home. How times have changed.

Take them with you...but don't forget to bring them back.

Reading/Story time

If holding a small child and reading her stories isn't one of life's greatest moments, what is? Kids become what they hear. Constant seeing and listening to the words of magical stories are lessons they will always carry with them. Imagine teaching children to read who were never read to. Now *that's* negligence.

* * *

This chapter surprised me. I felt it was going to be a little "fluff" piece on pointed hats, cake, and ice cream. But as I began to write and relive so many of the events listed here, I experienced an impact equal to any chapter in the book. That impact was the realization that family traditions and celebrations aren't just "things" we do. Instead, they are the very things that define our families, who we are, and what we will likely become...or have become.

You've heard it said that a chain is as strong as its weakest link. A child's ultimate security is his or her ability to resist negativity and temptation. Nature hates a vacuum. Don't jeopardize your kids by leaving them spiritually bankrupt. Create a lifetime of memories through a lifetime of family traditions.

CHAPTER 11

A CHAMPION'S
HONESTY

*I would give no thought of what
the world might say of me, if I
could only transmit to posterity
the reputation of an honest man.*

Sam Houston

Telling the Truth Matters

The erosion of America's cultural honesty has accelerated during my lifetime. What puzzles me is whether dishonesty is really on the rise or whether we're merely more tolerant and accepting of it. Clearly, dishonesty is blazing new trails in the political arena, our educational institutions, throughout big business, and within the very media we trust for truth and accuracy. When our institutions practice dishonesty, why should children embrace the importance of keeping *their* promises?

Honesty is integrity's foundation and character's anchor. According to Thomas Jefferson, "Honesty is always the first chapter in the book of wisdom." Dishonesty permanently stains our reputations and is not easily removed. Nor should it be easy given its influence on our character. The effort expended mastering either one is about the same. Both result from habits learned and practiced as children. That's why good fathers need to be above reproach in matters of honesty. Kids observe, learn, and quickly emulate the ease with which adults make empty promises and hollow commitments. "What's good for the goose is good for the gander" is a legitimate viewpoint if Dad himself fails to exhibit impeccable honesty.

A lie would have no sense unless the truth was felt as dangerous.

—Alfred Alder

Why Children—and Adults—Lie

I believe children, as well as many adults, lie out of some measure of fear. A troubling sub-factor on the rise is that they lie because they can. If the consequences of their dishonesty are marginal, it becomes easier, even desirable, to sidestep difficulties through untruthfulness. But fear is clearly the dominant factor among young people who lie regularly, and it takes many forms:

Fear of Punishment: A child so fearful of reprisal that lying is easier has probably experienced more *punishment* than *discipline*. Her main concern is pain avoidance. For many fathers, corporal punishment relieves them of sitting down and explaining why a certain behavior isn't acceptable. There's an old saying, "If the old will remember, the young will listen." Try it and you may be surprised.

Fear of Dad's Disapproval: Dad as teacher can inadvertently communicate the wrong message. Over time a child perceives his disapproval of certain actions and behavior. Reassuring them that the truth always trumps emotion would go a long way in discouraging this particular motivation.

Role Model's Example: Huge! Hands-down, the most important. We all agree that children will imitate and mimic at every opportunity. If they see you cheat, lie, or break promises, imagine the confusion and anger they'll feel when society punishes them for the same behavior.

Peer Pressure: Timeless and increasingly dangerous because today's stakes are so much greater. Lying to protect duplicitous friends suggests that the support and respect these peers provide exceeds the thought of disappointing you. No easy answer here but to roll up your sleeves and engage them.

Prestige: I know from my own childhood that these children lie to fill a void in their soul that's been blown open or never filled in the first place. Typically, these are the braggarts and loudmouths who equate volume with substance. They create an alternative reality, hoping to impress—desperate for respect and admiration. Doing everything you can to build their confidence and self-esteem as children is crucial. Fantasy can be titillating but reality is...well, real.

You can't force the truth, through fear or intimidation. It only encourages greater dishonesty. Truth and honesty thrive best in the warmth of sunlight.

To make your children capable of Honesty is the beginning of education.

—John Ruskin

Action Plan for My Children

Kids brought up comfortable in their own skin are children who were raised right. My kids are learning that who they are and what they represent take precedence over the opinions of others. Knowing God had a hand in all of this only reinforces their confidence. Being God, he's typically not prone to error. Affirmation that my children are uniquely special and supremely capable completes the package.

I now know that only honesty provides legitimate and long-lasting self-esteem that may otherwise have been sought through dishonesty. Humility has bestowed upon me more peace and security than vanity ever did. I now know that the less you think you need, the more you really have.

Whoever undertakes to set himself up as judge in the field of truth and knowledge is shipwrecked by the laughter of the Gods.

—Albert Einstein

Where We Are Today—and Why

Dishonesty has plagued mankind since Eve and the apple, but today's world is inching ever closer to a politically correct abyss. Undeniably, it is an exciting and exhilarating era where the confluence of events has aligned precipitously with the times. But black and white have now become gray. Traditional standards of ethics have become dynamic. Morality is being negotiated, event by event, and the truth is increasingly subordinate to the desired or wished for.

Commitment to honesty is surrendering to the practice of telling people what they think they want to hear. Candor is cautiously restrained, directness capitulates to evasiveness, and moral values and core convictions are falling victim to opinion polls! We are a nation becoming increasingly governed by whim and emotion instead of principle and purpose.

They say in war that truth is the first casualty. Could that same axiom be applied to today's big business scandals? Human nature's lust for power, predictably, follows the path of money. It was as true during Caesar's time as it is today. As in the past, justice will prevail and the cycle will begin anew.

Truth is beautiful, without doubt
. . . but so are lies.

—Ralph Waldo Emerson

Different Types of Honesty

No debate on honesty is complete without attempting to parse it into meaningful segments. "Being honest" has contextual differences depending on the circumstances. It's enlightening to explore the many faces of honesty...if only to recognize and appreciate their distinction.

Truthfulness

Who can forget the timeless image of young George Washington, axe hidden behind his back, responding to his father's question with, "I cannot tell a lie, Father. It was I who cut down the cherry tree." I think most of us would agree that, normally, telling the truth promotes trust and faith, while lying advances suspicion and scrutiny. Truthfulness seems the obvious choice.

Intellectual Honesty

Promoting a position or cause they know lacks truth or merit simply to promote their agenda is the personification of fallaciousness. I'll give you a good example.

My mother and father were exceptionally well-educated and otherwise thoughtful people, and they idolized President John F. Kennedy.

Years after his assassination, when an abundance of negative and unflattering information emerged about him that persuasively separated the man from the myth, my parents both refused any discussion of the possibility that it was true, that JFK was less than perfect, even mortal. Instead they trained their anger on the historians, and even *me* for being the messenger. I loved my parents dearly but I concluded, in this instance, that their behavior was dishonest and disingenuous.

Like my parents, many people are emotionally unable to disengage from their *emotional* position. They don't just <u>want</u> to be right, they <u>need</u> to be right. One look at election-year politics affirms the truth of this fact.

In human relationships, kindness and lies are worth a thousand truths.

—Graham Greene

"White Lies"

I recently stumbled upon a letter to the editor in the newspaper railing against the traditional practice of *little white lies*. My only rational conclusion was that this was simply the shrill ranting of some pointy-headed academic with too much time on his hands. I became more confident of my assumption as he raved about the immorality and lack of core values we promote by telling Grandma how great she looks wearing underwear outside her clothes and her hat is on upside down.

Please. Can we all agree that more value is derived than harm done by exercising kindness and discretion on such occasions? Raise your hand if you think it's a good idea to tell your wife—just returning home from a three-hour, $200 hair-styling appointment, "Gosh, honey, I'm so sorry about what happened to your hair!"

I wonder if the pushy little malcontent who penned that article includes Santa Claus, the Easter Bunny, and the Tooth Fairy in his moronic list of "frowned upon" embellishments. His kids must have had a ball growing up in that house!

Integrity Via Self-Honesty

Children need to be honest and accept who and what they are. Heck, we all do. Life isn't gauged by what we may become or achieve. It's judged by the effort and dedication we demonstrate along the way. It reminds me of a verse in the famous poem, "Desiderata," *Never compare yourself with others or you will become vain and bitter, for there will always be lesser and greater people than yourself.*

Emotional Honesty

It's impossible to separate all emotion from every stressful situation— but it's crucial to try. Ten people confronted with identical situations will respond in ten different ways. This indicates a choice in how we react to any given event. We can opt for rationale and reason, or launch a frying pan through the window. We can take a deep breath and gear down or decide to lash out no matter the consequences. We can elect to respond thoughtfully or lose control and say something we can never take back. Do we really want to be forever haunted by the look in a young child's eyes from witnessing something that he will never understand—or forget?

Integrity

Simple is always preferable, always better. To that end, Leah Arendt said, "Do not do what you would undo if caught." In other words, don't kick your golf ball into a better lie, never fail to give back the mistaken change the clerk gave you, don't take two newspapers out of the vending machine with one quarter, and for Pete's sake, stay out of other people's medicine cabinets!

It's unfortunate, considering that enthusiasm moves the world,
That so few enthusiasts can be trusted to tell the truth.
—Arthur James Balfour

A Closing Thought

A man unable to believe in himself is incapable of believing anything else. If the context of his life is dishonest he can never honestly evaluate the condition of his life. After all, the basis of integrity and character lies within our own ability to be honest.

I still keep in touch with that friend I have occasionally mentioned in these pages. While he was always a lovable and cuddly character who epitomized the "good times," he was cursed by his compulsion to lie and steal. Today his life is in shambles as he intermittently rotates between the world as he would like it to be and the world as it actually is—never being entirely confident or comfortable with either. He lacks honest self-appraisal and, while still likable, he cannot be trusted. It is the cross he bears from a life so void of honesty and integrity.

CHAPTER 12

A CHAMPION'S
DISCIPLINE

*Self-respect is the root of discipline;
the sense of dignity grows with the
ability to say no to oneself.*

Abraham J. Heschel

Discipline—or Punishment?

Generations of American children grew up with a healthy respect for the paddle or strap. I find no compelling evidence that spanking children is harmful when properly administered by loving parents. That said, I also find little evidence that spanking furthers its primary purpose of discouraging bad behavior.

Children generally benefit from loving parents committed to enforcing sufficient standards of behavior. Many five year olds are simply deaf to reason but not blind to discipline. Corporal punishment should be used sparingly but always have it as a readily available option. Convincing kids that bad behavior will invite swift and certain consequences is one of a father's most important jobs. If you don't demand their accountability ... society most certainly will.

In its function, the power to punish is not essentially different from that of curing or educating.

—Michel Foucault

John Wooden, Joe Dumars

My modified opinion on the merits of spanking surfaced after visiting both John Wooden and Joe Dumars. With eight children, Joe's parents rarely spared the rod when punishment was needed and every son I met on those visits had his own personal memories of those painful "whuppins." Yet each son also came to recognize and appreciate the love and high sense of moral purpose that motivated such harsh punishment.

On the other hand, John Wooden remembered spanking his son only once and doesn't remember ever striking his daughter. And while his viewpoint on the subject of discipline was different, his purpose was identical to the Dumars—unconditional love for their children coupled with unwavering commitment to their proper rearing.

Wicked men obey from fear; good men, from love.

— Aristotle

Different Methods—Same Result

The most notable similarity in these two families is the caliber of adults stemming from their respective children utilizing vastly different parental models. Listening to their stories of mischief and punishment I also noticed something else. To a man, their eyes betrayed the tremendous love they had for their fathers.

So what's the secret? The answer is simple if not difficult to accept. Love. That's it. *The absolute and unconditional love* of a parent renders the method of punishment and discipline (within obvious reason) moot.

The sting of the paddle subsides with time but parental love endures a lifetime. Not only won't they hold it against you—they'll come to thank you for it.

What lies in our power to do,
it lies in our power not to do.

—Aristotle

Teach Self-Discipline

Discipline is a two-sided coin. The flip side is *self-discipline.* Steering clear of self-destructive habits challenges every generation of young adults.

Self-discipline is a reflection of a child's inner strength and self-esteem. Inner strength and self-esteem are influenced primarily by the family's moral values. A father's credibility when preaching the merits of health is diminished if he smokes, drinks, and leaves the sofa only for work or bed.

Better to be pruned to grow than
cut up and burned.

—John Trapp

No Discipline: My Story

My own life is testimony to the difficulties awaiting an undisciplined child as an adult. Two loving and gentle people in their middle 40s adopted me when I was six months old. By any measure they were kind, decent, and loving. In contrast I was wild from the start, badly in need of a firm hand. I didn't get it.

Added to my growing list of problems was a high degree of intelligence and decent athletic ability. This afforded me substantial success at most things I pursued. Unfortunately it also acted as a catalyst for my bad behavior, accelerating my problems and their consequences. I was a 400HP engine with no brakes.

My life was characterized by excess and I eventually paid the price. Never learning moderation I spent most of my young life dodging chaos and crisis. Only when I married and had kids did I rein myself in and begin practicing meaningful self-discipline. Looking back I should have joined the Marines out of high school. I badly needed discipline and had nowhere else to get it.

Your kids have enough friends…be a parent. Their anger stemming from your discipline will pass—the consequences of an undisciplined life might not.

Lack of discipline leads to frustration and self-loathing.

—Marie Chapian

Are You Discipline "Training" Your Kids?

I draw often on the analogy of *"time invested"* with your kids being as important as the dollars invested for your retirement. Success in either is dependent on quantity and quality. To that end, I pose this question.

What do people do when pursuing important goals? Athletes? Armies? Actors? Cheerleaders? Marching bands? Any team sport?

They *TRAIN!* To achieve performance gains, they all must diligently *TRAIN!* Diligently. Vigilantly. Relentlessly. Persistently. They *TRAIN!* Is a child's future any less important? Shouldn't we practice discipline with the same zeal and commitment?

Strong self-discipline stems from the ability to practice from within. Rehearse in your mind. When your mind talks, your body listens. Self-discipline means holding your ground when you'd rather run away. It's counting to ten instead of lashing out emotionally. It lets you smile instead of scowl. It motivates harder training when you'd rather quit. It means drilling discipline into them. Challenge their goals and share their dreams as you help them achieve both.

I'm always looking for opportunities to praise my kids or otherwise build them up. At other times I point out things that will require more work and discipline from them. Their minds are training to think things through before responding. The message to fathers? *Don't be lazy.* Look around. Be aware of more than their *presence.* Constantly examine how your kids are living their lives. Only then can a father help them learn to live it better.

Anybody who gets away with something will come back to get away with a little more.

—Harold Schoenberg

When to Discipline

Too many parents stressed out from the pressures of their own lives take it out on their kids. Be it yanking them around the grocery store while criticizing and complaining the entire time or simply *hovering* over their kids, on the constant lookout for something to nit-pick or criticize. (Don't we all have someone like that where we work? They're called "managers.") Kids become defensive and a parent's credibility is diminished on those occasions when strong discipline is actually warranted.

Family rules will differ when serious discipline is called for and might include:

■ When their *continued* actions create a risk of injury to themselves or others, or damage to property not their own.

■ Any form of disrespect to any adult.

■ Aggressive action motivated only by anger or malice.

■ Unexcused shirking of designated and understood responsibilities—schoolwork, curfews, chores, etc.

■ Acts of deliberate dishonesty.

Your family's individual circumstances and dynamics will vary, but in principle these are among the most important.

He who lives without discipline dies without honor.

—Icelandic Proverb

How to Discipline

Teaching fathers how to exercise discipline is like suggesting there is only one way to make a Dagwood sandwich. Many factors play a prominent role.

My parents were devout disciples of the *"Don't spare the rod"* school of discipline. So what changed my mind? Two things. Having children of my own and a casual discussion on the subject with former UCLA basketball coach John Wooden. John Wooden was a great coach and also an instinctively gifted teacher. He gently but clearly explained the difference between discipline and punishment. I had always assumed the two were synonymous.

Punishment by definition, he said, is punitive and does little to change or modify bad behavior. Proper administration of timely discipline can't help but modify behavior. I found his viewpoint convincing and compelling.

So how would he exercise discipline? He would quickly *remove* what mattered most to the person or

157

persons exhibiting the unacceptable behavior. When his UCLA basketball teams practiced with insufficient effort or enthusiasm—he'd turn off the lights and go home! Without fail, these champion thoroughbreds returned the next day, raring to go. Had he responded in anger, berated them, and ordered extra laps as punishment, they would have simply become angry, and resisted any adjustments to their attitudes and behavior.

I tried this on my own kids and it worked like a charm! They misbehave—I simply tell them, "If you don't do this, I'm taking away that." Try it. It's simple and it works great. They learn important lessons without fear or anger. Yes, it works better than spanking.

Anticipate—Be Proactive

I owned a business that obliged me to study and analyze crime statistics. Rape! While shocked at the sheer number of violent rapes, I was more astonished by studies suggesting that 85 to 90 percent of them could have been prevented through minimal anticipation and preventative action. How many other tragedies could be avoided if people would just give thought to risk avoidance. Perhaps women working late could arrange to be escorted to their cars, not sleep with open windows or doors unlocked, etc. How many tragedies could we avoid but with thoughtful contemplation.

My point is, if risk avoidance is so effective, shouldn't parents be its greatest practitioners? Awareness is a father's utmost tool in preventing many of the dangers our children will encounter.

Survival in business frequently depends on how well managers respond to the unexpected actions of their competitors. Always look ahead—anticipate and plan! The expected will always be subject to Murphy's Law. The consequences are real. Always expect the unexpected and make allowances for it.

Self-respect is the root of discipline; the sense of dignity grows with the ability to say no to oneself.

—Abraham J. Heschel

The "Rules" of Discipline

- Exercise fairness and consistency.
- Get to the point quickly.
- Let your children give their side of the story.
- Ask questions—seek to understand their perspective. It's important!
- Seek their opinion and input on what they believe to be a fair remedy.

Try and do something fun and enjoyable together, as quickly as possible after the conclusion of the action. It's important to put it behind you and move forward.

Avoid . . . !

- Emotion (pursue reason).
- Conduct discussions and remedies in private.
- Do not be unyielding or unreasonable simply because, as their parent, you can.
- And finally, *don't bring it up again!*

A *torn jacket is soon mended, but hard words bruise the heart of a child.*

—Henry Wadsworth Longfellow

When Not to Discipline

A young, unemployed woman named Lisa used to do some housecleaning for me. She had a little four-year-old daughter and no husband. She wasn't the best house cleaner but she was pleasant and needed the money.

On one memorable occasion her daughter accompanied her to my house. Her name was Heather and she was so sweet and outgoing, I immediately grew fond of her. I got her a soda and she happily and eagerly began drinking it.

Predictably, the can of soda slipped out of Heather's little hands and spilled all over my carpet. Her mother shrieked, "G— !D——! Heather," swatted her bottom, looked me square in the eye while wagging her finger in Heather's sobbing face, and blurted, "Steve, this is exactly why you should never have children!"

It was all I could do to resist the impulse to shame her to tears. I quickly went and got little Heather a new can of soda, sat her on my couch and told her, ***"You know, you drank half of that soda before you spilled it. I usually spill mine just trying to get the can open!"*** Heather smiled and perked right up. I grabbed Lisa's hand and walked her outside for a talk.

I won't elaborate on *that* discussion. While I deplore any physical child abuse and would never tolerate it, I'm more convinced of the long-term damage inflicted by careless and cruel remarks from the people our kids love most. It does nothing but further undermine their already fragile self-esteem and confidence.

Temperance is a bridle of gold.

—Burton

The Greatest Gift

Watching my children grow up with the necessary confidence and good judgment to be successful would fulfill my dreams and expectations for them. There is no effort too great or sacrifice too large when teaching our kids to do the right thing. Instilling discipline will be one of your greatest callings—and challenges. Discipline is about keeping promises. Promises to others and, especially, promises to ourselves.

Our thoughts shape our world. The management of our own minds ultimately defines our lives. As Ralph Waldo Emerson once said, "That which we persist in doing becomes easier to do, not that the nature of the thing has changed, but that our ability to do so has improved."

* * *

SOME CLOSING THOUGHTS...
FROM ONE FATHER TO ANOTHER

God indeed works in mysterious ways. What began over six years ago as little more than a letter of introduction to my unborn child has become a labor of love that taught me how to be a better father. It was a personal catharsis as I finally broke free from the past and embraced a hopeful future with my wife and children. It has become an iron-clad contract between myself and my son and daughter. That contract stipulates that I will do the right thing always and try *never* to be absent when they need me.

Fatherhood is a serious job. Obviously too many men view it as some part-time job or other inconvenience. For me it's an honor that I struggle daily to be worthy of.

I grudgingly surrendered my adolescence in my late thirties. "The grass is always greener" had defined my attitude during those early years. Like so many of my generation, I equated the accumulation of pleasure with the attainment of happiness. I discovered just the opposite.

Happiness comes from humility and a strong sense of purpose regarding who you are and what your life means to you as well as those close to you. Long-term happiness is realized when your own spiritual well is so full that you can donate the surplus to others in need. Ultimate happiness is raising children that the world can be proud of when they become adults.

At the ripe old age of forty-six, no sound warms my heart more than the laughter of my kids. No smell is sweeter than their hair as I hold them in my arms. Nothing brings tears of joy to my eyes easier than the smiles and squeals they emit whenever I come home, or when I am kneeling beside their beds watching them sleep, wondering what dreams are dancing in their young minds. Perhaps my greatest pastime is being present to observe the wonder and fascination in their young eyes when they see and experience so many of life's treasures for the first time.

Time is life's great equalizer—we're all rationed equal shares and will be ultimately judged by how we use them. Good fathers donate the lion's share to the welfare of their growing children. It's an investment that will make you rich beyond your dreams, leaving behind a legacy that no amount of money can purchase.

Professional football players have a term for that rare instance when a player's performance transcends his talent, exceeding all expectations. With reverence and awe they would unanimously salute the player with a heralded proclamation, "Man, he sure as heck left all of it on the field today, didn't he?"

When my time here is over, I hope the life I gave my children elicits something similar.

"Man, Dad sure left it in our lives . . . didn't he?"

—— ORDER FORM ——

To order additional copies of *To Father an American Champion*, photocopy the order form below and mail it with your check to:

> American Champion Publishing
> 9227 Lincoln Avenue, Suite 200
> Lone Tree, Colorado 80124
>
> You may also order online at www.USAchampion.com
> or call the publisher at (303) 791-7055.

Discount schedule when ordering directly from the publisher:

1-2 books	**No discount ($14.95 each)**
3-4 books	**20% ($11.96 each)**
5+ books	**40% ($8.97 each)**
Sub-Total:	_____

Shipping & Handling ($3 for first book and $1 for each additional book)   _____

Total Enclosed: _____

Name _____

Street _____

City, State, Zip

_____

Phone: _____ **Email** _____

Please allow 4-6 weeks for delivery. Call for information on overnight or express delivery. Thank you for your order!